141 Days:

Bike for Christ

Michael T. Baker
with Matthew E. Morgan

141 Days: Bike for Christ
by Michael T. Baker
with Matthew E. Morgan

Some scripture taken from the NEW AMERICAN STANDARD BIBLE®, Copyright © 1960,1962,1963,1968,1971,1972,1973,1975,1977,1995 by The Lockman Foundation. Used by permission.

Some scripture take from THE HOLY BIBLE, NEW INTERNATIONAL VERSION®, NIV® Copyright © 1973, 1978, 1984, 2011 by Biblica, Inc.® Used by permission. All rights reserved worldwide.

Some scripture taken from *The Message*. Copyright © 1993, 1994, 1995, 1996, 2000, 2001, 2002. Used by permission of NavPress Publishing Group.

DEDICATION

Little did I know that once I gave my life to Christ (started to follow his teachings), my life would never be the same. From the day I acknowledged there was a God and that He loved me more than I could ever know, I started to be taken care of in a way that I could never imagine on my own. This book about my journey could only have happened through God blessing me in ways I never would have been able to put together on my own. I owe much gratitude to the people God used to help me through the process of completing this book. It was one of many other blessings that God threw my way.

It all started at Gahanna Christian Academy, where I spoke and shared my testimony. I was able to meet Chris Joseph, the principal. Over lunch, I told him I had two journals about my trip that I wanted to turn into a book. I mentioned that I started writing it myself but lost motivation soon after the 5th page. He quickly replied, "I think I know someone who could help you. Want to go meet him??"

I, of course, was very interested and jumped to the opportunity— trusting in God's planning and not my own. He took me back to the school and introduced me to Matthew Morgan ... after pulling him out of a class that he was teaching. We exchanged in a small conversation about my desires for a book and from there, God started putting it all together. I can't explain enough in words how thankful I am for Matthew in putting in so much effort to make this possible. Praise The Lord. Without Chris Joseph, I probably never would have met him.

God can use anyone to put his plan into action. I am truly Blessed.

~Michael T. Baker

ACKNOWLEDGMENTS

This book is in itself an acknowledgment—a testimony of what God can do when people dedicate their whole hearts to Him and yet do not lose sight of the needs of the people around them.

'Love the Lord your God with all your heart and with all your soul and with all your strength and with all your mind'; and, 'Love your neighbor as yourself.'

Luke 10:27 (NIV)

CONTENTS

1 THE DARKEST NIGHT

I thumped on the ground, my bicycle clattering next to me. My backpack flipped lightly—nearly empty of all my supplies. I surveyed my surroundings through my sunglass frames, having taken the lenses out so that I could see in the pitch blackness and yet have something to hold my rear-view mirror. My helmet clunked hollowly against the building behind me as I drew my legs up, fighting exhaustion, loneliness, and cold. I looked around for a better shelter, but the blackness of the late night air hid any solace. The only sign I could read hung from the campground entrance: "Closed for the season." It might as well have said, "Go away, Michael Baker. Turn around and go back. You're not going to make it." I shivered against the cold of the night, feeling icy tendrils wafting in the air—pointing the way home, taunting me to quit.

I wanted to oblige them. I was less than halfway into

one of the most difficult climbs of my trip: 4000 feet upwards spread over 20 miles. It would have been much easier to turn around and head downhill. My journey did not lead that way, however. I had spent over a third of the year 2011 on my bicycle traveling across the country, having planned to travel from Ohio to Connecticut to Florida and then San Francisco, California. More than just that, I wanted to attempt it with as few possessions as possible, so when I left Ohio I had only $300, my bicycle, and some basic camping gear and supplies.

Now, my gear and the trailer that had carried it were gone, shipped back to Ohio to remove my option of staying put. It also enabled me to travel this 317 mile stretch as fast and light—and with as few stops—as possible. I had no money and only a pittance of food left. Breathing as deeply as my exhausted lungs would allow me, I looked up at the stars in the night sky, and searched desperately for an answer.

This hill was not my first hill; I had been up difficult ones before on this trip. During those times, I had friends by my side who cheered me on, encouraging me not to stop. They offered accountability as well as safety. But they had gone their own ways, following their own paths.

The cold I felt was not my first exposure to exhaustion or danger. I had seen it all before on this trip as I fought through elements: heat, wind, and rain. I had felt such fatigue in my legs that I was not able to take another step.

And I had been in harm's way more than once—to such a great extent that I wondered how I would escape. Every time one of these situations arose, rides had come to carry me through it or new friends found me and offered me shelter and supplies. But this stretch of road lay before me solemn, lonely, and unyielding. It offered no escape, comfort, or solace. No cars came. I sat alone.

After shivering my way through a few hours of restless sleep, partly because of the elements and partly out of fear someone would kick me out of the area, the sun rose the next day. I continued to press onward, too far into my journey to turn back; my journey was all I had. My legs had quit screaming at me about the pressure I had put on them, and instead felt numb. Yet, they did not dictate my trip. I pushed them 81 miles through the day. Part of the way through, I dialed a number on my iPhone, trying to connect to part of an organization that offered hospitality to cyclists, but I received no answer. I continued to press onward through the setting sun and into the night, until my phone showed me it was 2am. My throat tight and sore, my sinuses plugged, and my legs exhausted, I looked for something to use as shelter long enough to catch a short nap. I found a construction site with 3-foot culvert pipes stacked three high. I forced my exhausted body to climb to the top one, comfortable it would keep me safe from the elements, as well as the animals roaming the night. I forced my eyes to close, and they did.

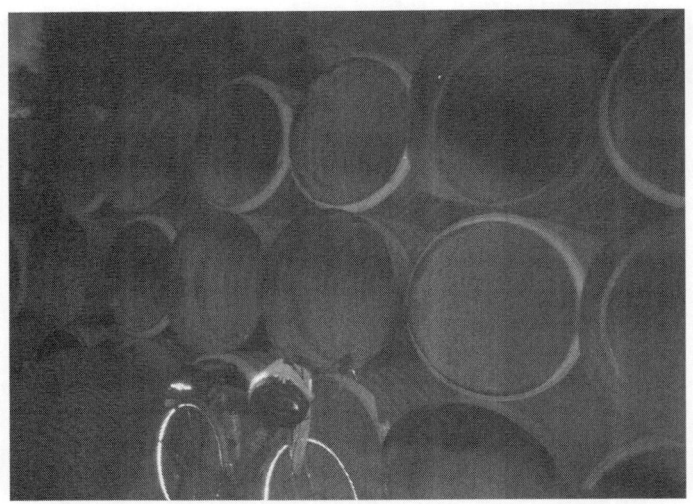

The pipes in which Mike spent the night

Four hours later, I awoke with a refreshed feeling and some renewed excitement, knowing I only had to make it 50 miles—a cakewalk compared with some of my previous trips. There had been days in which I had rode over 100 miles with relative ease. Unfortunately the euphoria of the day's plan and my four hours of sleep wore off quickly. As soon as I started to pedal, a strong headwind met me. In a car, headwinds are uncomfortable. For a cyclist, they are detrimental. These, however, weren't just the average headwind—the gusts easily topped 30 to 40mph. Considering I probably rode at an average of 10 to 15 mph, progress did not come. The gusts ripped past me. If I was lucky, I managed to stay on my feet. If I was really lucky, it only slowed my progress to a crawl. With no other choice, I forced myself to pedal through the resistance, each step taking so much effort that biking even just a few feet brought excruciating pain to my legs. During the harder gusts, I had to focus all of my effort on keeping my bike upright—rather than moving. Finally, feeling nothing but frustration and exhaustion, I stopped and put my head down on my handlebars.

I had to make a choice.

I could just give up. I had accomplished a great deal already. No one would have looked down on me for stopping when I did. These conditions were difficult for anyone and I had so few resources left to deal with them. I had already experienced so much, meeting new people and experiencing new things. It could still be a victory even if I didn't make it all the way to San Francisco. Giving up was definitely the easier choice.

The harder choice was pressing onward. I had learned one major lesson on this trip. Instead of focusing on what I didn't have, I needed to praise God for what I did have. When I started out this journey, I had found a scripture that had carried me through many of my trials, "I can do all this through [Christ] who gives me strength" (Php 4:13). God had carried me through so many difficult situations—ones that might have been impossible under different circumstances. He had sent me friends— sometimes ones who shared the journey with me and other times ones who had offered me respite from it. He had provided food, water, shelter, and from complete strangers. God had kept me safe through accidents and from potential ones. I looked down and remembered I had not started the trip out with this bike. It had been a blessing of epic proportions—more so than I would have ever thought to ask. More than just material needs though, God also allowed me to see so much of the United States—good and bad, ugly and beautiful. He had also worked on my soul and my thoughts. As I had traversed much of the country, I had tremendous chances to read my Bible, pray, and commune with God. I was not the same person who had left Johnstown, Ohio all those months ago.

My exhaustion, my lack of money and a place to stay, and even my hunger were all things God had helped me with before. I knew He would work something out. He always did and He always does. I pulled out my iPhone and dialed another number as I mentally thanked God for all the ways He had been with me through this trip.

2 THE JOURNEY OF 6000 MILES

Lao-Tzu, a Chinese philosopher, said "A journey of a thousand miles begins with a single step." Granted, my "step" was more of a pedal, but the sentiment was the same. And it was fitting—even though my journey would surpass the 1000 miles of *The Way of Lao-Tzu*. At this point of my trip, I didn't know by how far I would exceed it. When I set out, my original goal had been to make it to Middletown, CT and see my friend Conrad. It was definitely a far journey - 800 miles - but I enjoyed the challenge. In the back of my mind, however, I had a pervasive thought … ride to San Francisco. It was a crazy thought: I was ill-equipped and I had never attempted anything even remotely that big. But I imagined people who climbed mountains, ran races, and overcame personal adversity often had the same thoughts.

About the beginning of April 2011, I came up with the

idea for my bike trip. I wanted to do something where I took a long trip and lived on bare essentials, getting rid of all my debt and having no bills. I even thought about getting rid of my cell phone to make sure I had no attachments to the world. I couldn't think of a better way to do that than get on a bicycle, travel the country, and live off the love of God through people. I also wanted to build my own faith and see how well God would take care of me. The trip was set.

I started sharing my ideas with people and most of them thought I was crazy. They asked me things like, "What will you do for food or sleep? How will you pay for this trip?" They asked me if I was an experienced cyclist. I had done a little mountain biking but never any road or long distance.

It seemed only my good friend Conrad and my brother Tom were all for it. Conrad gave me the moral support I needed and Tom and his wife told me they would pay for my cell phone so I could keep it running.

I set a date, started a blog, and began journaling. Paying off the last $3100 of my motorcycle debt felt so good. I also started gathering supplies and gear. I bought my tent and sleeping bag. I even practiced with them by sleeping in the yard. My tent wasn't huge—just enough room to give me some shelter from the elements and keep my gear dry—but it would do the job. About two weeks before my departure date, I had bought my bike and I was determined to hit the road.

This trip reminded me of when Jesus sent out 72 disciples in groups of two (Luke 10). He told them to take nothing extra—no bag, purse, or even an extra pair of sandals. They were just to go wherever life led them, being sure to preach and do miracles wherever they landed. He never promised everything would work perfectly—in fact, He gave them a reminder that when they were rejected, they were not to take it personally. They were not being rejected, but Jesus was. Here I was, trying to live out that project in my own way.

The first ten miles down the road, things seemed surreal. Though the road was familiar, I knew it took me further from my home. My parents, my brother, and all those who supported me were drawing farther away—but they could still come to me in no time. The emotional high of the first several hours started to melt with the warming of the day. In fact, I had to stop for a moment and pull off my sweater; the morning chill had dissipated quickly in the beautiful early May air. Looking back, I pretended I could see the 10 miles back to where I started.

Sunday had seemed like a good day to start. I had ridden my bike to church and attended the service. Afterwards, a group of about 25 gathered to send me off in the best way possible—with prayer. I remember kneeling in the midst of them, tears flowing as I realized the immensity of what I was about to undertake. I had no idea what to expect in the future, but in that moment I felt like I could do anything. There were no words to describe how I felt with the support of these people around me. Their words had strengthened and encouraged me before I had even taken the first step. As I had felt the cross necklace dangle from my neck, a perfect picture of love—Jesus on the cross—I listened to the most amazing prayer I had ever felt—and would be the first of many prayers on this trip.

Before I left, I had gathered once more with just my family and my close friend, Mike. For those who get the idea to follow in my footprints—or bike tracks—please know that Mother's Day is not the best day to leave home. Even though I was 24 years old, I was the youngest of my siblings, and I'm sure the thought of me leaving home for an indeterminate amount of time with virtually no possessions to my name did not make my parents feel at ease. In retrospect too, I might have made it more difficult on myself, because I hadn't told anyone about this trip until about a week before I had planned to leave. I knew people would talk me out of it by putting doubts in my mind—and this trip was supposed to be about building my faith.

So I tucked my sweater into my backpack. I looked down at the necklace and gasped. It was gone! I sighed in frustration; I had barely started my trip and already the devil was trying to break me down. I decided not to let it upset me and continued onward. The necklace wasn't going to take care of me; Jesus would. It was nice to have the physical representation, but Jesus wasn't on the cross. He was alive, active, and working with me to develop a stronger relationship with him.

Forty miles into my trip, I started to climb some hills—the first of my trip. Bicycling cross-country isn't like a road trip in the car where the driver jumps in, sets the cruise control, and just keeps the car between the lines. A cyclist can feel the subtle hills a car driver hardly notices. Cyclists also have to worry about terrain. Things can change quickly. Rocks, sticks, and even animals (dead or alive) can turn a casual ride hazardous. Debris cars roll over without consideration can be seriously detrimental for bicycle tires and spokes. There would be many times a small piece of metal, a sharp stick, and even a larger rock would bring my trip to a temporary halt as they punctured my tires.

Today though, the road was smooth and the weather was perfect. The sky surrounded me with gentle blue warmth and a refreshing breeze kept me cool. I knew things wouldn't always be this way. I wouldn't always be close to shelter when weather hit. I wondered what I would do if the weather turned severe, but then again, there was little I could do about any of that.

I also found a challenge I hadn't considered—the

struggle to keep my mind occupied. I couldn't pop a movie in the DVD player and put the bike on cruise control. I had some music on an iPod to keep me company, but I also needed to keep my ears open to anything around me that I might need to hear. At least the ride provided me with ample time to think.

Those thoughts whirled through my mind as my spokes turned. The most predominant, as the sun began to set and my legs started feeling some exhaustion, was where I was going to sleep. I had my tent, but it wasn't like I could just pitch a tent on the side of the road. In some places, laws prohibited that; in other places, common sense prohibited it. A tent didn't provide the greatest amount of security against any predator—animal or human.

As I had left church that morning, Pastor Larry had told me I could look for the "Church of Christ" denominational signs. Many of them would be likely to offer me hospitality. Just as the fatigue in my legs started to get overwhelming, I entered the town of Killbuck, OH and saw a sign ... literally. A sign with an arrow pointing down the next road read, "Church of Christ."

"Maybe there might be someone there to ask to camp," I thought. My worst case would be that I could just set up camp there anyway and trust God to provide. I figured I'd rather be on a church property without permission than any other land.

Five to 10 miles later I came up to the church property, which included two houses as well as the church itself. I thought they might belong to the church, so I decided to ride up and ask for permission to stay. The nerves in my stomach started a workout to rival the muscles in my legs. I felt so nervous talking to complete strangers that I just passed the first house without even stopping.

The setting sun reminded me the day was drawing to a close and I was running out of options. I pulled up to the second house and dismounted my bicycle. I started walking towards the door, but before I even reached it, a man opened it and greeted me. I took a deep breath and introduced myself. Ed did the same. I told him my situation. He and his family were eating, but they invited me right in to join them. I was amazed and truly blessed to have come to this place. I had plenty to eat and they said it was no problem to sleep on their property. It was such a relief to have a place to stay.

God had even more in store for me though. Ed called the preacher of the church, Bobbie. It didn't take long for Bobbie to come over; he lived in the first house on the property—the one I had passed. He and some others arrived and I had the opportunity to tell them all about my journey and my plans for the trip. There were about ten people altogether and they all seemed interested in everything I had to say, not taking their eyes off me while

I spoke. We all ended up in a circle, while Bobbie prayed for me. I loved that my day had started and ended with prayer. In fact, for the next two months, Bobbie would call me about once a week just to check and see how I was doing and continue to pray for me. He also encouraged me by letting me know his church was praying for me as well.

As I had been sharing my story, I thought about the Irish bards of medieval times. These musicians and storytellers would travel the land, acting as chroniclers, heralds, or simple entertainers. Here I was, with no income and no intention to stay stationary long enough to earn one. I did have a story. It was only a small one at this time, but the longer I spent on the road, the more it would grow. Little did I know, as I shared it with a small group of people in Killbuck, OH, this story would carry me to places I had never been, meet people I never would have met, and do things I had never done. As I had done when I had approached Ed's doorstep, I just had to be brave enough to speak it.

As the sun set over a beautiful view of the countryside, little did I know this one stop would be the start of a new routine for the next five months. There was no doubt in my mind: God had blessed me right from the start.

The next morning I woke up and stowed my gear. A

strange feeling passed through my gut as I thought about my "new normal." Things had changed so much in one day. "Making my bed" consisted of rolling up my sleeping bag and packing my tent, making sure I didn't leave anything behind. I still brushed my teeth and freshened up for the day, but now that included putting on sun block, as I knew I would be out in the open sun for its entire trip through the sky. I still put on shoes to go to work—but they were now cyclist shoes. The strangest difference was that my only goal was to follow where the Lord led me.

Once I had packed, I put my feet to the pedals, continuing towards my first goal: Middletown, CT. It seemed so far away; I hadn't even reached the end of Ohio yet. Using Google Maps on my iPhone, I found a route for bicycles and started down the road.

Google seems to think all bicycles are created equal, and I can't say I blame it. I used to think that as well. When I started preparing for this trip, I had done no research on bicycles. I had done some mountain biking and knew that wasn't the best bike for the trip. I went to a bicycle shop just before my trip and they sold me a Gary Fisher road bike. As the name suggests, it was great on the open road. "Open" is the key. As I bounced across the gravel and dirt roads, it jarred my spine terribly. Just as I reached the point where I wasn't sure how much longer I could take the punishment, my bike gave me a break. Unfortunately, it also gave me a flat tire.

Flat tires are part of the cyclist's journey—and a well-prepared cyclist keeps several tubes on hand. Having a spare tube is only half the battle, though. Even though it's a fraction of the size of a car tire, a bike tire is still quite difficult to change. In the past, I had changed few tires on my mountain bike, but during the first part of my trip I quickly became an expert at it. Changing a flat started by taking the tire off the bike. Then I used a special tool to pry the tire off the rim. When I first started changing tires, I would just take the old tube out and pop the new tube into the tire. I learned, thanks to the cruel mistress of experience, that it is essential to inspect the inside of the tire for damage. Too many times, metal splinters from car tires that had blown out on the road caused my flats. The splinters would stay in the tire and subsequently puncture the new tube. I also learned the hard way that I needed to air up the tube a bit before putting it in the tire to help it take shape. Then I had to use the tool to slip the tire and tube back on the rim—without puncturing the tube. If I successfully did all that, then I only needed to have the hand strength of a professional arm wrestler to pump the tire back up to 100psi. At the start of the trip, it took me about 10–15 minutes to change each tire. By the end of my trip, I would be able to do the same process in about three minutes.

With a new tire on my bike, I wanted to find a

replacement for the spent tube as quickly as possible. Nothing would bring a faster stop to the trip than a popped tire with no spare. Fortunately another cyclist had come by and told me where the closest bike shop was—5 miles ... in the wrong direction. It was getting late in the day and I figured I should play it safe, spending the time and effort to get the new tube.

It turned out to be a positive gamble. Not only did I buy the new tube, but I had talked to Ernie, the owner, and he let me camp on the shop property. With two nights under my belt now, I had not yet lacked for a place to stay.

With my new morning routine finished, I hit the road again, feeling fortunate to have two nights of sleep behind me. Now that I knew what I was in for, my mind had even more to ponder during the first 50 miles of riding that day. As the night grew closer, I started looking for a place to camp. I expected asking complete strangers for help would have come easier to me, but it was still a new skill. I wondered, *How does one go about asking a complete stranger to sleep in their yard?* I figured my best strategy was to just start off by asking people how they were doing and going from there. I could follow up with, "I have a crazy question for you" or "You probably have never had anyone ask you this but..." Regardless of how I got there,

I knew I would have a chance to tell my story in exchange for a small section of grass on which to sleep.

I started looking for people to ask. An older gentleman was working in his garden. I stopped and told him the quick version of my story. He was polite but suggested I might have more luck going down another street to the park. As it wasn't on my direct route, I just opted to continue onward.

I knew there was some risk. I wasn't in a populated city. Country roads had virtually no traffic and the houses came infrequently. I did find another house a couple miles down the road with a gentleman working on his truck. As soon as I started talking, five dogs began barking. He said staying with him probably would not be a good idea since the dogs would bark all night long. I understood, thanked him for his time—over the barking of the dogs —and continued down the road.

This was a different scenario. Lodging for the last two nights had happened so easily that I hadn't considered what might happen if people said no—and it just happened twice in a row. Feeling the worry start to creep in, I prayed aloud. "God, if you want me to stay on someone's property, I want you to put them in the middle of the street. I want there to be no doubt in my mind that you want me to talk to that person." It was a specific prayer to be sure, but I had faith God would answer it. Part of me thought this showed a lack of faith, but then I thought about Gideon in the Bible. He was unsure of his calling, and prayed that if he left a piece of wool outside, in the morning it would be wet and the ground would be dry. He did the same thing the next morning, but in reverse (Judges 6). God didn't condemn him for that, so it must have been okay.

God did answer my prayer ... exactly. Riding only about half a mile more through the sparsely populated country roads, I suddenly saw a young kid—probably 5 years old—standing at the end of his drive yelling at the top of his lungs.

"Lemonade stand!"

I immediately laughed as I thought about how I had asked for someone to be standing in the middle of the street. Here was my answer! Well, of course I wanted lemonade. I pulled over and bought my cup as an older boy came out of an RV parked in the driveway. He had just finished packing it up.

I asked if I could talk to the homeowner and the boys went and got their mom, Denise. I told her I was riding my bicycle to build my faith in Christ and the faith of others and asked if I could camp in her yard.

"Why don't we put up the RV?" she said.

"That would be awesome!" I said.

God continued to bless me through this stop. Not only did I have a place to stay, but she invited me in for dinner and gave me a chance to take a shower—one of those conveniences people don't think about … until they can't take one. Not only that, but she had also just bought a new blender and some whey protein, and she offered to make me a shake. After her husband came home, he promised me a good breakfast in the morning as well.

As we talked, I found out just how big of a blessing this stop was. The boys had actually started the lemonade stand without permission—while Denise was sleeping! I had been one of the two customers of the day; a back country road with a 50 mph speed limit was not exactly a prime location. As I got ready to turn in, they told me they had plugged in the RV in case I needed power for anything—which I did, since my phone battery was low.

Keeping a phone charged would be a challenge during the trip. Normally, at home, I would plug it in while I slept. My tent didn't exactly have a power outlet. Instead, I had a solar panel zip-tied to my helmet. The panel would charge while I rode, provided the sun was strong enough that day. If not, I could always plug it in and use it as a battery. In the evenings, I would discharge the solar panel into the phone. I also learned to take advantage of my rest stops—gas stations, restaurants, and the like. If they had a place to plug in, I would always make sure to do so. My phone was my lifeline. It worked as my GPS, my weather map, camera, video recorder, and—of course—it was a phone too. Almost every night, I would call my family and let them know I was still safe.

That night in the RV, I certainly felt safe. Even though it stormed badly outside—with thunder, lightning, and down-pouring rain—I smiled, feeling safe and comfortable from my bed in the RV.

Was God really going to take care of me like this the whole trip?

3 THE WRONG BIKE

The next two weeks were filled with adventure. I had some great "up" moments ... and some rougher ones. One day, I had put in about 50 miles when I suddenly realized how lonely I had felt. I have always had friends and family around me. I'm the youngest of four brothers, and—as is typical when guys get together—excitement was always brewing at my house. Being on the road was completely different. Here, it was just me. As the empty feeling in my gut grew, I found myself not quite as excited to continue onward. The temptation to quit gnawed at me. Just as I thought about calling it a day, my phone chirped. I looked down to see a text from my mother:

Just remember when someone tells you 'no', that means GOD has better things for you ahead. Love you and keep on biking.

Tears of joy flowed down my cheeks—the perfect words at the perfect time. She gave me strength to push on another mile … then another two miles … and then another 32 miles. Just as that burst of mental and physical energy started to diminish, I met Rebecca—who had been outside watering her plants—and Evan. Not only did they offer me a place to stay, but they let me rest my legs while they took me on a tour of Presque Isle State Park in their car. The park is a beautiful peninsula of Pennsylvanian land jutting into Lake Erie. It amazed me to see water, beaches, and greenery so close together. After the driving tour, Rebecca and Evan took me out to Five Guy's Burgers and Fries to eat. In the morning, they fed me a great breakfast. Those meals were such a welcome break from my typical one—which lately had been a NuGo bar smeared with some extra peanut butter. It was a far cry from a gourmet meal, but it had the protein my muscles craved.

At the end of the next day's ride, I met Dianne, who let me camp in the picnic area on the property next to her. The campsite was beautiful: a flat piece of wooded land nestled amongst 50-foot cliffs on three sides. A creek wound along the cliff base, providing a beautiful view and a soothing sound. The only thing that could perfect this scene would have been having a nice campfire crackling outside my tent. I knew biking across the country would be a survival situation, so I had taken the advice of one my favorite survivalists, Bear Grylls. I had seen him start enough fires, so I did what I needed to do. I assembled a small hut of kindling, keeping the bigger logs close by. I brought out my Bear Grylls knife—a great survival tool for someone in my situation. The knife has a sharpener, emergency whistle, survival guide, and a fire starter. Taking a deep breath, I tried my hand at starting a fire from scratch.

It was a good thing I also had a lighter for backup.

The next day, I couldn't wait to reach Niagara Falls, NY ... but I would have to. About 30 miles from the falls, another flat tire waylaid me. Determined not to let it get to me, I sighed and started to change it. I was getting to be good at this process and my confidence showed as I hummed along, working through my tire-changing process.

I should have known: the new routine was that there was no routine.

I had filled my tire up about half way when I heard a crack from the pump. Air hissed from the wrong parts. I had broken it. And the air I had managed to get in the tire was not enough to support the combined weight of my gear and myself. I was still riding right on the rim. *What good could possibly come from this?*

If I would have had the time to pray for a miracle, I would have asked God to send me someone with a bike pump. Before I even had the chance, God had already sent Marty—another cyclist on his way up to the falls. Unfortunately, he hadn't grabbed his pump that day, but he did know the area—including the location of the nearest bike shop. As we made our way there, another cyclist passed us—and this one did have a pump. With the extra air, we arrived and I was able to pick up another pump ... and also a spare tube to replace the broken one.

After my repairs and replacements, it had grown late and I still had 20 miles to the falls. Normally it wouldn't have been a big deal to wait, but the forecast called for rain for the next several days and I wanted to see the falls without feeling them.

God always found the most interesting ways to answer my prayers. Marty took me to his daughter Amy's house and the two of them actually drove me to the falls. Later they fed me dinner. Afterwards, Marty invited me home and put me up for the night, blessing me with a shower and a nice soft bed. The morning brought another incredible comfort ... apple pancakes!

And as nice as the material blessings were, Marty also gave me some indispensible help. Part of undertaking this journey meant trying something I had never done before. As with any new activity, there was bound to be a learning curve. Even with my limited cycling experience, I had never undertaken such a long trip—and distance drastically changes things. I made a number of mistakes due to my inexperience. But it's been said that "God watches over fools and children"—though I prefer I Peter 5:7, "Cast all your anxiety on [God] because he cares for you" (NIV).

Indeed, God loved me so much that He sent an experienced cyclist like Marty to help with this leg of the trip. First, Marty showed me maps of where I should go, including Albany, NY—where his son lived and would be happy to put me up for the night. Second, Marty gave me some saddlebags for my bike to help stow some of my gear. And third, he gave me advice I had never thought about: like wearing waterproof gloves when it rains to keep my hands warm and lining my saddlebags with trash bags to make them waterproof.

He also gave me some bad news too—about my bike. As I said before, my only biking experience had been on a mountain bike and I knew that wasn't the best bike for my trip. I went to a bike shop, expecting to get knowledgeable help. That's when they sold me the Gary Fisher road bike. I thought I had received a great deal, paying only $900 for it.

As it turns out, in the world of bikes, there are three types: road, touring, and mountain bikes. The road bike they had sold me wasn't made for long distances plus heavy weight—which was exactly what I had been doing to it. It had smaller tires and an aluminum frame. It also didn't have all the gears one would need, since it's mainly built for speed.

Had Marty sold me a bike, he said he would have recommended a touring bicycle. With its larger tires and steel frame, it would withstand the abuse I gave it. The touring bike also had more gears—and in particular, the lower gears that are indispensible when climbing. Frustrated, there was little I could do about this at this point of my trip other than trust God to help me through it. My hope wasn't in my bicycle—it was in God.

As soon as I continued my journey the next day, I felt just how big of a blessing the saddlebags were. Getting the weight off my back made a huge difference in my stamina and energy. Realizing the right gear helps the journey so much, I stopped at a bike shop to get a rack for my bike, which would help distribute the weight of the saddlebags even more. Unfortunately, I found another difficulty with my bike was that it wasn't set up for racks. Despite that limitation, the bike mechanic was able to make it work.

This left me with an old rack that I wasn't sure what to do with. I certainly wasn't about to carry it the whole trip. I could have tried to sell it, but I had been blessed with so much I wanted to be able to give it away. My path led me to Don—a cyclist sitting at a church with a flat tire waiting for help to arrive. We spent some time talking before I gave him my old rack and continued down the road.

I had hardly gone a mile when Don pulled up beside me in his car. I thought for a moment he might offer me a place to stay. After all, God had done stranger things already on this trip. Instead he just asked me how much farther I was going for the day and then drove onward. With that door closed, I wondered what God had in store. I remembered my mom's words: when God says "no" it's always because He has something better in store for me.

As I biked onward, my path crossed Don's again. This time he had pulled off on the side of the road. As I passed him, he flagged me down and insisted on me staying at his house. Praise the Lord! He hadn't asked me the first time because he had been talking it over with his girlfriend. Another "chance" meeting brought me dinner, shower, laundry—and a movie! And of course, it also gave me a comfortable place to sleep.

The next day, Don took me to his church. It was the first time I had been to a Roman Catholic Church, and it was an amazing experience. Afterwards, we enjoyed lunch together, but the day got away from us, so I ended up spending another night with him. It amazed me to think a man who had been a perfect stranger a day ago was willing to house and feed me!

I left the next morning in the midst of sprinkling rain.

Again, something simple in normal situations completely changes a cyclist's life. When I rode through the rain, I needed to reorganize all of my gear to make sure the important things stayed dry. The saddlebags helped with that somewhat. I also had a pouch compartment with a waterproof cover for my phone. Once my gear was safe, I had to protect myself with all my rain gear. It was more than just an inconvenience to be wet, I could face sickness, chafing, and all sorts of other problems if I wasn't careful. So with my gear safe, and me as dry as I could be, I pressed onward.

Until another flat tire stopped me.

All I could do was praise God, so I decided to use the opportunity to take a little break. I pulled over at a gas station and rested on a bench. I felt slightly down; I knew I needed better tires. I couldn't keep going on like this, having to stop constantly to repair them. I also didn't like the idea of spending my limited money on them. And if that argument wasn't sufficient, I liked the idea of traveling back to the bike shop even less. The closest bike shop was 10 miles back the way I had come, which equated to 20 miles of riding with no gain on my trip. As I sat, wondering what my next step would be, my phone chirped out a notification that I had a voicemail. My good friend Ron McCarty had called to check and see how everything was going. I returned the call and told him about my circumstances. He said his spiritual mother—a close friend who had been influential in his Christian life—lived in New York ... and could probably help me. I contacted Pam, and he was right! She connected me with her friends John and Susan, who were 22 miles away from me—in the right direction— and would take me to a bike shop to get new tires. I patched my flat, jumped on the road, and met them a short ride later. They also fed me lunch and dropped me off at the bike shop.

I bought a pair of $113 tires—leaving me with $60 to my name. It frightened me to see 80 percent of my money gone so quickly into the trip. At least I had everything I needed. After our trip to the shop, Pam had me set up to stay at her son Doug's house. I was able to get a shower, a warm meal, and prayer support from a fellow Christian.

This is probably a good place to add a point of fact: I think I might be the pickiest eater in the world. My friends and family would also attest to my eating habits. They watched me grow up eating basically spaghetti, chicken, beef stew, and my mom's famous tacos. Later, I developed a taste for Chipotle and prior to my trip, I ate it at least four times a week. So to add one more life-changing challenge to the trip, I promised myself I would eat whatever people offered me. At the time, I had no idea I would be in and out of as many people's houses as I would be, but it proved to an interesting promise. Susan made the first chicken pot pie I had ever tasted. Granted, after riding around 80 miles a day, I would be hard pressed to turn away any food, but it just so happened that this food was delicious. I even wanted seconds.

The blessings kept coming the next day. Doug had a brother, Shawn, about 80 miles away—right on my path. Shawn said I would be able to stay with him. It brought an interesting challenge since I had to make a longer ride than I had been doing. Having a place to stay, food, shower, and laundry facilities, served as a great motivation. Once again, God blessed me with a perfect meal in the morning. After I ate and was ready to leave, Shawn and his family gathered around me and prayed over me and my trip. This was starting to be a regular thing. I was learning how powerful it was to have people praying for me daily. Even better, after we prayed, he handed me a hundred dollar bill to help with the trip. I had not mentioned I was short on money—but God used Shawn to provide. I truly couldn't have asked for anything else.

Each day seemed to work in the same pattern: challenge followed by blessing. One day I fought a headwind, riding in lowest gear the whole time. Yet, at the end, I met Donna and her husband and they let me camp in their yard. Every time I started to get down, something came along to lift my spirits. I checked my email one morning to see words of encouragement, "Keep your head up. God has something great for you tomorrow. I know it!" Shortly after I read that comment, my brother Guy texted me and said, "I woke up with a weird feeling that today is going to be an amazing day for you. Go get 'em!" Talk about a sign from God! I was so excited to see what God had in store for me, so I started the day with great expectations.

Nothing extraordinary happened, however, and at 5pm I figured I should start looking for a camp site. I passed a grocery store first, where I bought some bagels and turkey. Outside the store, I sat down on a bench, made some sandwiches, and ate them. As I ate, though, I noticed a bicycle path. Even though I had already mapped out my route, I figured I would check to see where it led. The worst case scenario would leave me camped on the side of the path or in the woods.

Instead, I found a house with a man outside. I took a chance and asked him if I could camp on the property. His aunt Dianne actually owned it, so he called her and asked. She was fine with me camping there. In addition, she was an elder at her church, and she and about a half-dozen other elders were having a meeting that night. Diane invited me to meet them and tell them my story. It was such a blessing just to be able to share what God had done.

When I finished, they still had church business to discuss. Dianne offered to take me out to dinner later; however, while they were still meeting, Dianne's nephew's wife brought me dinner—two hot dogs and a bag of chips. It looked like I wouldn't need Dianne's dinner invitation after all. If that was all God wanted to do for me that day, that would have been amazing.

Part of my routine for the trip was to call my mother nightly to let her know I was safe. Yes, I was 24 years old, but she would always be my mom. If I missed calling home, she'd probably panic. In addition to calling my mother, I decided to call my brother Guy and share my amazing day. After all, it was an answer to the message he had sent me earlier.

However, after the elder meeting finished, two women handed me money—one $100 and the other $50! I hadn't told anyone I was down to my last $20 and I hated the idea of asking for help. I was so excited to find out I didn't have to ask for money; God knew when to take care of me. They also said I could sleep in the church— a much better alternative to my tent.

The blessings didn't stop there, though. Even after being given $150 and a better place to stay (I loved sleeping in the sanctuary next to a giant picture of Jesus Christ), Dianne brought me an egg carton pad to sleep on. I had to call someone! I called my mom, my best friend Conrad, and my brother Guy. Around 11:30pm, my brother Guy texted me and told me to check my email. He and his wife read a prayer from a prayer book to their 5-year old son Brooks every night. He attached a copy of the prayer and said, "You will never believe what I randomly flipped to in the book on the first attempt. No more needs to be said."

The passage was a prayer that talked about the new opportunities given to someone when he or she leaves the comfortable and familiar and steps out into the unknown. Though it's terrifying, faith in Jesus as a companion makes it much easier. That prayer fit my situation perfectly. As soon as I read it, I laughed with excitement and praised God for His glory. The picture on the page was a family packing boxes as they were moving out of a house and a boy on a bicycle riding down the driveway. It was so similar to my situation! Praise the Lord. I went to sleep thinking about how great it was to witness how great God is every single day. I felt like my eyes had been opened to something new. I knew if I kept my mind on God, He would continue to show up in all the right places.

That was the moment I made the decision to head towards San Francisco ... just to see how much God could do during the trip.

Riding across New York brought more blessings. Marty had called his son Jon, so I had a place to stay there, as well as a shower. Jon didn't have much - I could see that from his refrigerator. Here was an interesting chance - the ability to provide for someone else. I ordered a pizza for us to split. In the morning, Jon made pancakes and eggs for breakfast! One of the best parts was having another Christian for conversation. During the day, the road tended to be lonely. Stopping with people who enjoyed talking about the things I loved as well was a tremendous uplifting to my spirit.

Not everything was perfect. Hills had started to increase in both size and quantity. At one point, my GPS brought me to two roads that didn't actually connect, so I had to carry my bike and all my gear up the hill. One of the simple truths I learned during this stage of my journey was: "No matter how many miles it takes to get up a hill, you always get to come down—and it's worth it every time."

The miles to Middletown ticked away as I travelled. As I drew close to having less than 100 miles left, I started feeling excitement. I was exuberant ... I was thrilled ... I was soaked. The rain poured down around me. I stowed my phone—which doubled as my GPS—to keep it safe in the storm. It stayed safe in my travel pouch ... meaning it was good and dry when I pulled it out to see the words "NO SERVICE." Those two words meant I had no map to guide me through this unfamiliar territory. I did the only thing I could think of - I just kept riding.

Finally, I found a slight signal, called my mother to tell her not to worry, and camped in a clearing for the night.

It was not the easiest night—the driving rain had subsided, but had soaked everything in the area. But I figured I had to suffer to appreciate the good things. As a reminder, I stumbled on some stones—a memorial about 100 yards off the road— where six people had died in a car wreck in 1934. I hadn't considered mortality, but here the simple fact stood in front of me. Human life is fragile and we never know when things may change ... or end.

The next morning brought a few more hardships. I woke up to 18% battery life on my phone. Even though it was charging on my solar charger, it was also roaming—which drained the battery. I rode on in faith, coming to a gas station where they let me charge my battery a bit. Again, God's timing was infinitely better than mine. While I was waiting on my phone to charge, I had a chance to share my story with five motorcyclists—each of whom gave me a couple of dollars to help support my trip.

My rough day behind me, I pushed on towards Middletown. The sights became more familiar; I remembered them from the four months I had lived there. Since Conrad, the friend I was staying with, wasn't home, I stopped at one of my favorite pizza places—and ate a whole 14-inch pizza by myself. It was delicious!

A few short miles later, I was at Conrad's house— enjoying hugs and a place that would be home for weeks—not just for a night. With 800 miles under my belt, the experience was amazing. I thought of Jesus, talking to Thomas—his disciple made famous for doubting his resurrection. Jesus had told him, "Because you have seen me, you have believed; blessed are those who have not seen and yet have believed" (John 20:29 NIV). I hadn't seen the people who had been praying for me, but I knew they had been out there asking God to keep me safe.

Looking back at the first leg of my trip, I knew I had been blessed immensely. I had received money, supplies, food, places to stay, and even company.

Some people might call that chance.

Some people might call that luck.

I'm going to call it love.

4 THE LAST TIME I CROSSED THE COUNTRY

Seeing Conrad again brought a flood of memories. He and my older brother Tom were actually best friends in high school, so they hung out a lot. I was included by proxy. As the years passed, Conrad and I started to build on our friendship, which really took off after Tom moved out to California. Our personalities meshed well.

As we started to explore future careers, I had one of my first big life adventures with him just after I graduated high school. Conrad and I determined we were going to be filmmakers, so we packed up and moved to Los Angeles to be with Tom, who had moved out there to be an actor. I wanted to get into film editing and Conrad loved writing and directing. Together we all wanted a part of the film industry. Movies had been a big part of our lives. We thought it would be amazing if we could make our own realities. We knew movies were an incredible outlet—a good movie could inspire people to do something great. Movies also allowed people to experience new realities and take on different lives while they watched them.

We started the journey to LA: Conrad in his 92 Toyota Corolla and me in my Ford Ranger, both eager to start the 2,254 mile, 36 hour drive. We said our goodbyes and set off on our quest. Everything went great for the first half of the drive—until disaster struck in Albuquerque, NM. Conrad's car broke down, leaving us stuck on the side of the road. We waited three hours in 100 degree heat for the tow truck to arrive—which we found out was actually the second tow truck. The first one had broken down on its way to retrieve us. The truck dropped the car off at NAPA, but it was Sunday and they were closed, so we thought we would have to wait until the next day. We just hung out and were playing cards when the shop owner arrived. He invited us back to his house, but we declined, not sure of what waited for us. Instead, he gave us the option to stay in a RV that had been sitting on the property for quite some time. We took the safer option, even though the RV had some fire damage and probably had not been updated since the 60's.

The owner of the shop was confident he could fix Conrad's car at first, but after diagnosing it, he told us the computer had short circuited. He wouldn't be able to get a new one. With few options, we condensed our packing, put all of Conrad's belongings into my truck, stayed the night in a hotel, and then continued to LA. Conrad would later buy a computer and ship it to the shop so they could fix his car.

We arrived in LA about midnight and connected with Tom—who showed us the three-bedroom apartment he had rented for us. The good news was that we found a place in our budget. The bad news was that it was in North Hollywood—a pretty bad neighborhood. Determined to make the best of the situation, we unpacked some of our belongings and then went to sleep.

Within the next couple days, Conrad found a computer for his car and sent it to the mechanic—only to find out it wasn't the problem and the car couldn't be fixed. He was stuck in Los Angeles with no vehicle— multiplying the challenges of finding desirable work to pay the bills.

We had a few assets—about $12,000 worth of film equipment, including a Canon XL2 DV camera and a PowerMac G4 editing computer. Through some interesting circumstances, we paid considerably less for it than it was worth. Unfortunately our liabilities seemed to be far greater: no jobs, limited transportation, and a city with a terrible reputation in finding work.

Looking at our situation, we decided to sell the camera and buy Conrad a vehicle. That was one of our first mistakes. Selling the camera was like a carpenter selling all of his tools to get a work van. He might be able to get to the jobs, but he wouldn't be able to do them without his tools? Our inexperience and impulsiveness winning out, we sold the camera and bought Conrad a Honda RC51 sport bike.

For two years, we survived in Los Angeles—though we did not survive well. We tried to stay focused on our filmmaking goal, but our finances made it difficult. Tom found some work as an extra as well as some other acting gigs. Conrad secured various jobs in the film industry. I ended up doing an internship for a special effects company. Despite the small successes though, the struggle to survive eclipsed our vision, drastically changing our motives and desires. We all got lost in the world.

It was a good thing God had different plans for all three of us.

The party lifestyle distracted me—mostly behind the wheel. I never transferred my license to California, but my Ohio license racked up plenty of tickets. Even after a judge suspended it, I still missed my court dates. People should not miss court dates; I learned that lesson the hard way. I ended up with a bench warrant for my arrest— which meant if the police pulled me over, they were supposed to arrest me and take me to court. Apparently, LA cops have bigger things to worry about; they pulled me over numerous times with that warrant and never arrested me. They even let me go after I had received more than my fair share of warnings. These were not minor traffic violations. I had bought a motorcycle and Tom, Conrad and I had fun speeding around the city and racing the canyon roads. I had tickets for going 160 mph and not having insurance, a current registration, or a driver's license. My immaturity at the time showed; I would rather ignore my tickets than take care of them.

Looking back at that time in my life, I'm surprised nothing terrible happened to me or others. I never had an accident—even though I wasn't remotely worried about getting hurt or dying. I was just trying to have fun. I think God was looking out for me then. It's interesting to see how God uses situations that seem negative to us to actually help. For instance, I parked my bike one day in a fairly nice neighborhood—Sherman Oaks. As I returned, it sickened me to see it was gone. Someone had stolen my motorcycle right off the street! I had only had it for about a year and a half. So many bad choices hit me at once. It was a 2006 GSXR 1000—a $13,000 motorcycle. Since I didn't have credit, I had bought it under my mom's name. In retrospect, I almost wish she had told me "no" about the loan. The interest rate was high—close to $10,000 over the life of the loan. In other words, $23,000 just drove away. To make matters worse, I had been too broke to afford insurance so I had to continue making my

$300 monthly payments through the life of the loan—
even without the motorcycle.

I wasn't the only one with legal problems. Tom had
been a personal assistant for a man named Andrew, a
millionaire. Tom and Andrew became friends, and
Andrew helped Tom through some of his financial
problems. After a while, Andrew wanted repaid for the
money. To help Tom pay him back, Andrew cosigned for
a $20,000 credit card and Tom would make his payments
to Andrew on the card. After a few months, Tom was
unable to pay and it impacted Andrew's credit negatively.
Andrew's attorney advised him, in order to save his
credit, to file identity theft and grand larceny—both
felony charges.

The next time Tom got stopped for speeding–which
didn't take long with our track record—he was arrested
and spent 35 days in the Los Angeles county jail. I visited
him a few times, but it became clear our Los Angeles
adventure had drawn to a close. Conrad moved back
home to Connecticut with his parents, where he still does
film writing and works on local projects. I moved back
home to Ohio with my family ... except Tom.

He joined us later.

Well, someone who looked like Tom joined us. While
in jail, he spent most of his time reading the Bible. It
changed his life. My brother had always been known as
being a bit crazy. He was a partier and a troublemaker

until he got saved. Things changed then: he went from being a sinner who drank and partied to being a follower of Christ and wouldn't even allow himself to say a swear word. He went from living a party lifestyle to working as a youth minister at our church. I had never witnessed firsthand someone changing their lifestyle so quickly. Fortunately the criminal charges against him were dropped. The prosecutor's attorney decided she wouldn't represent Andrew because she didn't believe the charges; however, God already had ample time to work in Tom's life through that situation.

Me, on the other hand, I took a little longer to change. After moving back, I went to work for my dad again—doing handyman work and installing ceramic tile and hardwood floors. However, because I had not taken care of my California escapades, I had no insurance and license. I hated having to drive illegally, but I needed to be able to make a living. Those days taught me about guilt and how much it affects a person. It showed up as fear; every time I passed a police officer my stomach would plummet like the first drop of a roller coaster.

Finally, with Tom's encouragement, we took a trip back to Los Angeles. Tom wanted the chance to see Francis Chan at his church in Simi Valley. I wanted-or rather, I needed-to go stand before a judge and take care of my traffic violations so I could get my license back. Unfortunately for Tom, Chan left his church and we didn't have a chance to meet him. I was a bit more successful. I went to the courts and waited an hour for them to open. Normally I would have had to wait for a court date, but since I was traveling, I could pay the fines in full instead. It took all the money I had saved: $1300.

Eventually, after paying the fines, reinstatement fees, and getting my license back, I ended up paying around $2300, an extremely painful and expensive lesson. I had to return to driving with a learning permit, and then I had to retake the written driver's exam. Yet, with my penance paid, I finally earned my license back. I felt almost as good as I had the first time I received my license. I knew I could drive the streets again and not be scared of being pulled over.

This was where Ron McCarty entered my life—the friend who sent me the text about good things happening one day. Ron and Tom would constantly talk to me about my beliefs and try to convert me to Christianity. At the time I didn't want to hear it. I was content with my life and thought my beliefs were good enough: I was a good enough person and I didn't need anything else in life. It was like my driver's license. I thought if I just acted "good"—like I did by paying my fines and working to re-earning my license—then life would all work out for me. The more and more they preached to me; the more I didn't want to hear them.

Amongst all the sermons they preached, one thing

grabbed my attention and wouldn't let go. I was riding in Tom's truck when he turned to me and said, "Mikey, if I could tell you one thing it would be that 'God is Love'." That was enough to get me to start thinking about Christianity as a way of living. The rest fell into place from there. Tom introduced me to Francis Chan's sermons online and I fell in love with his style of preaching. He just spoke plainly about God; he was easy to understand and yet made me think about who I was and what I was doing in life. He was so influential on my early faith.

As I started opening up more to learning about God, I began going to church with my family. I even bought myself a Bible—though I didn't read it much at first. As the weeks went by, my dad started to push me to be baptized in water. I turned him down—mostly because I didn't really know what baptism was about. I started researching it and learned it was an outward sign of my inner change. It was strange to see that there wasn't anything really mystic about it. When most churches baptize people, they dunk them under water and bring them up again. The process is a way to identify with Christ, since He was buried and resurrected.

With that knowledge, I felt more comfortable seeking baptism. My father ended up being the one who baptized me. It was a good experience-and I loved how everyone congratulated me after it was over. I guess I expected it to somehow change me; however, I went back to my lifestyle just a few days later, though I continued to attend church every Sunday. Everything was going good but I still felt like there was something more I needed to find in life.

Even while attending church and watching Francis Chan videos, I still didn't feel like I had the faith I wanted. I didn't even consider myself saved until May 8th, 2011—the day I started my trip. My trip gave me the chance to see what God was truly about. It was about living life as a new creation that follows the ways of Christ—leaving my comfortable lifestyle and changing my ways. I knew God and Jesus Christ were by my side. God reaffirmed that fact every day of my trip through answered prayers and love through complete strangers. God was in my life more than I have ever felt before, and I was more confident of that than I had ever been.

Arriving at Conrad's house brought all that back. I was glad that even in the midst of my new life, I still had pieces of the old. Conrad and I had been through so much together. I'd like to say we just sat down and talked about deep theological issues; however, that would not be completely true. We did talk, but we also did what we're best at—experiencing life together. We went climbing rock faces and rappelling back down. We also did some work together to make money.

My time in Middletown reminded me of a basic truth

in life. We all need rest. I heard a preacher once say that God made the world in 7 days—6 days of work and 1 day of rest. He said an omnipotent being doesn't "need" to rest, but He did need to set a pattern for all his children. The Bible calls the rest day a Sabbath, and this time with Conrad was a well-needed one. The rest time helped me in a couple ways—other than the obvious benefit of having a steady place to stay for a little bit. It gave my muscles a chance to recover. It let me get work done on my bike—hopefully to be a more effective rider. It still bothered me that I had the wrong bike, but there wasn't really anything I could do about that in the middle of my trip.

The rest did give me a chance to add two things to my journey. I ordered business cards that just had my name, my blog, and "Bike For Christ" on them. I figured the card would show people that I was serious about my trip. It would also be a chance to leave something with people so they could follow me and what I was doing. I also made a waterproof sign to hang on my back that read, "Bike For Christ." Again, I wanted people to know what I was doing—and more importantly, for whom I was doing it.

Unfortunately, as all rest time does, my time with Conrad had to end. If I was going to get to San Francisco, I couldn't take too much time. Having to go through mountains during the fall season would be uncomfortable—or even dangerous--the later I waited. Even knowing that, though, it took all my willpower to leave. It was difficult returning to the fray after having rest and relaxation, but I knew I needed to do it.

5 OUTER BANKS ON MY OWN

Saying goodbye to friends and security all over again, I left Conrad and the rest of Middletown on June 4th and headed towards New York City. I had wanted to get at least half of the 100 miles under my belt, and I made 82. It was a great day of riding, ending in Greenwich, CT. I could tell there was a lot of wealth in the community and I'll admit I felt a little excitement about where God was going to put me that night. All the houses were large and well-kept. I asked one person if they would give me a place to camp. He turned me down immediately. A second person did the same thing. I wasn't worried; I'd been down this road before.

As I rode along, I saw a business-type man pull into his driveway and I thought, *Here's the place I'm going to stay.*

He opened his door. I took a deep breath and said, "Excuse me."

Immediately, he grabbed his cell phone, waved it in my direction and said, "I can't be bothered right now; I have to make a business call."

He didn't even give me a chance to speak.

I figured this wasn't the right community to ask for favors ... and it was starting to look like rain. It was such a cliché situation that I wouldn't have written it into a movie. Yet here I was, feeling a little rejected, so I went and pitched my tent in a park, hoping no one would find me. It wasn't the best location, but I was on an island so I thought I should be as safe as I could be.

I went to sleep, but at 1am, the sound of a truck engine close to my tent awakened me—not a sound anyone wants to hear, let alone someone in my situation. I felt some fear in my gut and quickly prayed for God's protection.

"Hello?" I called out.

"Police!" the voice called back.

I felt a mixture of relief and dread. Taking a deep breath, I did what I had been doing all along: I told my story. The officers told me the park closed at dusk and I wasn't supposed to be camping there, but they took my information and let me stay.

It couldn't have gone better!

I woke up early—6am—pumped and ready to go, with

only 18 miles to New York. By 9am I was sitting in central park, enjoying the sights and sounds of New York City. The hustle of the city was a far cry from the rural sounds I had been hearing. It was musical, though. People talked, their conversations overlapping in every direction. Cars and other vehicles made a symphony of noises with the engines, horns, and other sounds. Buildings stretched higher than I could see.

I tried not to think about some of the more pressing concerns on my mind. I was back down to $20 to my name. I knew I would be okay for the next few days; I was meeting my friend Greg here. We hadn't seen each other in about four years, so it would be fun to catch up. We connected at a gas station and he bought me a Gatorade. Back at his place, we hung out and played video games, Then he indulged me in one of my favorite treats—Chipotle! Praise God! It was one of the best foods next to pizza—which we had the next night ... after riding his dirt bike around the yard most of the day. It was fun to be on a bike with an engine for a change!

The next day, I knew I had to be hitting the road. My time in Middletown showed me it was easy to get comfortable and forget about what I was supposed to be doing. Fortunately, Greg had some work to do in Pennsylvania, so he offered to drive me there. It was a great start to get out of the city. The jumpstart came with a drawback: we had to be up at 4:30am. Still, by 8am I was 50 miles from Philadelphia, PA—a ride that should have been easy to do.

It must have been the lack of sleep—or possibly the rest I had taken--but my legs burned terribly as I struggled up the first giant hill. I tried to push the pain from my mind, knowing a nice downhill waited for me on the other side. When I reached it, I enjoyed the long coast ... for a bit. Then, I started feeling a wobble in the back tire. Before I hit the bottom the wheel grated against the frame loudly. I felt the frustration well up. Here I was coasting downhill on what should have been the easy part of the ride, and suddenly my bike just broke down! I didn't hit any potholes, it just seemed to bend on its own.

As I inspected the tire closer, I found the culprit: a broken spoke. Those little pieces didn't look like much, but they were crucial to the tire. I glanced up at the sky, tempted to be angry about my situation.

My reaction surprised me! I realized how quickly I had forgotten all the ways God had blessed me. I bent the wheel back the best I could, and tried to continue onward with determination. It was hard to stay motivated, though.

I knew that the best way to keep a strong faith is to constantly think about God. Christians need to always read their Bibles and seek God with all their hearts. The problem starts when they take their eyes off God; that's when sin enters. Once sin comes in, it breeds more sin, which pushes the presence of God away and results in less love. Christians always need to have their thoughts on God and always need to be building their relationship.

Realizing my faith had been tried, after 30 miles I chose to stop and rest ... the right way. I read my Bible and prayed for a bit. Afterwards, I continued riding, but in about 10 miles I found myself in a really bad neighborhood. I had been in uncomfortable situations, but this was probably the worst neighborhood I had ever seen (and this is coming from someone who lived in north Hollywood). There were a lot of people in the streets—and all of them seemed to be staring me down as I rode by them. I stayed in constant prayer and kept the confidence that God would take care of me. I had to ride another 20 miles to find a decent place to camp—which was in the circle of a freeway exit, surrounded by trees. It was a strange place to find solitude, but it worked.

The next day brought more challenges. I took a quick inventory of my food and supplies: a couple of energy bars, five Pop-Tarts, and less than $10 to my name. Still I felt God would take care of me. I made it another 30 miles towards southern New Jersey and set up my tent in the woods. Seeing a big lake close by, I thought I might go for a swim. Two bee stings changed my mind. I climbed into my tent and called my brother, Tom. He put

$20 into my bank account to help me out. Praise God! He also gave me a new perspective on my trip. He pointed out that most of the blessings from the first leg of my trip had come from asking people to stay with them. I thought about it and realized I hadn't interacted with people since my difficult ride through Greenwich, CT. It might have been time to reverse that trend. It reminded me that the Bible calls Christians the body of Christ. That makes us his hands and feet.

The next day I woke up, determined to communicate with more people. I rode to a lake with the idea that I could use it to cool off, clean up, and hopefully meet some good people while I was there. A "No Swimming" sign greeted me instead. I rode a bit further and found the park office—where I met Greg. I ended up making a great connection there. We talked a little about my gear. It interested him because he was planning a hiking trip. He let me use the facilities at the office to take a shower before I hit the road.

That day I made it to the Delaware Bay. There was no tunnel, and a trip on the ferry was $10. It was pricey for someone with my finances, but God had been blessing me so much I figured it would be worth it. It was! I had the chance to hang out in air conditioning—a benefit I used to take for granted until I found myself pedaling through temperatures in the upper 90's. I also had the chance to eat while still making mileage—another combination of things I hadn't done in a while. The best part about my excursion to the concession stand was that, since the food had been sitting for a while, the worker gave me two slices of pizza for the price of one. I told her about my trip and gave her one of the business cards I had ordered in Middletown. I also picked up a recommendation on a campground at which I could stay.

On my way to the campground, my sunglasses broke. Again, something seemingly so minor as a pair of sunglasses was a major deal to someone in my place. Not only did they help me see in the glaring sun, they also kept my eyes safe from debris and insects.

After arriving at my destination, I kept riding around trying to find the office—apparently one of the campground's best kept secrets. I started to get frustrated, so I stopped on a bench to take a break. I looked down and saw a pair of sunglasses with no owner! It was unfortunate for someone else, but fortunate for me. I prayed God would bless the girl who lost them. Yes, the "girl" ... my new-to-me sunglasses were a pair of white designer sunglasses - complete with gold designs. They served their purpose well though.

After resuming the search for the elusive campground office, I passed a couple walking their dog and asked them for directions. Better than that, they let me stay with them … and they cooked me dinner, as well as pancakes the next morning. They sent me off with their card and told me to look them up if I was ever in Colorado. They also gave me a bunch of dry instant mix food. I felt God with me once again—and it was in the company of generous people. I hated to admit it, but Tom had been right.

The days weren't without challenges. At one stop, a park ranger yelled at me for walking through marine life (there were no signs posted telling me to keep off) and threatened to fine me just for making footprints. I encountered a few storms and a lot of rain, so I tended to tent myself in during those times. The road also threw a few challenges at me. At one point, the nice 10 foot shoulder I had enjoyed dropped to only a foot wide. After the first few cars and trucks passed me and nearly knocked me off the road, I figured it might be wise to walk a bit and slogged through some underbrush for several miles. On the other side I noticed I had picked up about 15 little hitchhikers—ticks—crawling up my shoes, socks, and legs. I picked them off, remembering something about Lyme disease being spread by ticks. I prayed, trusting God for His protection just like Paul did in Acts when he was bitten by a venomous snake (Acts 28). Speaking of dangerous animals, I also camped in an area I found out later is a popular hunting ground for bears and bobcats—the kind of hunting where I am the prey.

I realized something through these experiences. As bad as things were, when I reached San Francisco they would all pale in comparison to the joy I would have. It made me think about eternity. For the Christian, time on earth is Hell. For the lost, this is as good as it will get for them.

Despite the difficulties, the blessings flowed. I found a camp on an island—right on the beach. It was such a beautiful location that there was only one vacant spot out of 250. And I really didn't have the money to pay for it. That's when my brother texted me. He put $60 in my account and said he thought I was going to stay someplace sweet! He was right—the spot was sweet ... but the sight in the morning was even more awesome. All of the campers in the area, myself included, awoke to a family of four wild horses just outside our tents. Two larger and two smaller ones walked around, playing and rolling in the sand.

God continued to provide. Doug, with whom I had stayed some time prior, texted me and let me know he had a cousin in Virginia Beach and I could stay with him. My brother Guy told me he would be in Orlando about the time I was supposed to arrive there. He said I could stay with him ... in one of the classier hotels in Orlando since he was staying there for work. Having a place to stay was always a huge relief. Plus it gave me a goal–

which is a bit easier than just riding.

I also found spiritual comfort. Some of the campgrounds at which I stayed had impromptu church services on Sundays. At one such gathering, I had a chance to share my story and distribute cards. One guy at the service warned me about a tunnel I was coming up to in about 100 miles. Cyclists weren't allowed, so I'd have to hitchhike. He kept asking me what I was going to do when I got to the tunnel; I just kept saying I would hitch a ride. He told me he was too concerned I would get hurt so he insisted on taking me across instead. He drove me the entire way to and through the tunnel—and he bought me lunch!

With the time I saved, I was able to make it to a worship service at a Church of Christ that evening—arriving with time to spare. I met Howard tending the yard at the church and started a conversation with him. He took me back to his place, loaned me a pair of shorts, and took me to the neighborhood pool to go swimming! I had wanted to swim for a while.

We returned to the church, and I enjoyed the service. Right before the pastor closed, he announced who I was and told people to come up and meet me. It caught me off my guard, but I still had a chance to tell my story and pass my cards on to about 10 people (of the 60 who were there). One lady gave me her information and said I could stay at her house. Another couple said I could stay with them. Not only did I have a place to stay for the night, but I actually had options! Howard took my bike to the couple's house—George and Alana. They made me dinner and breakfast, and of course I had a place to shower and sleep. They let me stay in a warm and comfy guest bedroom. Praise the Lord

Normally, money might have been a concern as well. When I rolled into town I only had $10, however, Alana gave me $30 from the church as a blessing and my mom texted me to let me know someone at our church gave her $100 for me. Praise God, I was starting to understand what it meant to not worry about tomorrow. God was amazing.

I continued my journey, never lacking a place to stay. As I settled into a campground, trying to straighten another bent spoke on my bike, I started thinking about what Tom had told me. "Mikey, if I could tell you one thing it would be that 'God is Love'."

I had been turned away by people who didn't trust me or just flat out didn't care—many of them had a lot to lose. Other people, who had little to start with, gave to me with joy. The only thing I ever asked for was a place to lay my head, and God continuously used those people to bless me over and above that.

God told us to love Him and love our neighbor as ourselves. He also said to love our enemies. I have to conclude this is because everyone wants love. I thought about prostitutes—girls who are out looking for love, but never find it. I remembered watching a documentary that said the majority of these girls come from orphanages. My heart broke for them. They were just looking for love. In fact, I think everyone who does some sort of evil just wants some form of love. We as Christians ignore them because they make us uncomfortable.

I think that's why people ignored me early on in this leg. I knew my hair was getting longer, and the scruff on my face is starting to show. That could be part of it. The more I thought about it though, I realized how isolated we are as people. We don't talk and share lives together. We come home, open our garage doors remotely, drive inside, and close them behind us … without ever saying hello to a neighbor. I wondered if I would have driven 100 miles for someone in my church the way someone had done for me. It would have been so easy to let me go and hope someone else would take care of the situation, but he had taken the time to care about me as a person.

I decided then I was going to try to talk to everyone I saw on this trip. *Good things happen when we come together.* I learned that lesson from the people I had met on the trip, as well as from the people back home praying for me. I didn't take this trip out of some need for salvation or to reach a quota for God. I did it because He loves me.

I thought about things from God's perspective. What if I was God? I created the earth, people, nature, and everything else. Then they fall. They sin. They do the one thing I asked them not to do. Yet, I have it all planned. All I have to do is sacrifice my Son—part of myself—so they don't have to suffer wrath. It's not just death—it's a painful, sacrificing death, all for humanity's sake. I take care to record that—and so much more—in a book that is passed along from generation to generation. I record miracles upon miracles—trees growing, hearts beating, and lungs breathing. And when I go to them, tell them what happened, they ask me for another sign. How would I react to that? When is enough, enough?

The difference between me and God is that I'm not perfect. It was easy to get sucked into this idea that I had to work to find God's approval. I had to stay strong and remember God was there to help me. I needed to ask, seek, and knock. I needed to put my doubts to rest—not worrying about tomorrow and instead focusing on what I was doing that day. The worst case scenario might be that I would die—but even that was not the end. It would be the beginning of another adventure, starting with the words, "Well done, good and faithful servant" from Jesus.

6 FINDING FRIENDS

It's better to have a partner than go it alone.
Share the work, share the wealth.
And if one falls down, the other helps,
But if there's no one to help, tough!

Two in a bed warm each other.
Alone, you shiver all night.

By yourself you're unprotected.
With a friend you can face the worst.
Can you round up a third?
A three-stranded rope isn't easily snapped

Ecclesiastes 4:9-12 (The Message)

This passage in Ecclesiastes really exemplified how my trip had gone. I didn't have a right to complain: I had already been blessed by so many people who provided temporary relief. On the other hand I had felt some of the excitement of the trip started to wane. Combining that with some of the close calls I had with harm already, and I was really wishing for someone with whom I could ride. It would have been nice to have someone to "pick me up" if I fell. In the back of my mind, I knew something bad could happen. Having multiple people provided a sense of safety. Even if my trip went smoothly, companionship would have been heartwarming. I missed the encouragements others gave me. Another person would provide perspective to the present situation. Multiple people also provide safety—something valuable beyond measure on this trip.

The bottom line was that I felt vulnerable by myself. I knew God was on my side, but it would have been nice to have a physical reminder of that.

God answers prayers—and in such big ways. It probably shouldn't have surprised me anymore, but it still did. At one of my first stops, I was about an hour early waiting for the scheduled arrival of a ferry to take me across one of the waterways. The ferry ended up being an hour and a half late. But God has timing for everything. Because it took so long to come, a group of four bicyclists were able to make it on the boat. We started talking and I told them I was heading towards Florida. As it turned out, so were they—and they invited me to join them!

Frank, Adam, Joel, and Joey were bicycling for a charity called "Gift a Bike" - a program that provided underprivileged kids with bicycles. Frank was a youth minister in Immokalee, FL. Every year he, Adam, Joel, and Joey would bike to and from a different destination, finding sponsors who would donate per mile. This year, they had gone to Kitty Hawk, North Carolina, and were on their way back.

I noticed they only carried a little gear with them. When I asked them about it, they told me they had an RV traveling with them. Sometimes it would ride along with them and other times it would drive ahead and find a place to stay for the night. And—praise God—since I was now riding with them, I had the chance to stay with them as well.

Biking with the guys brought all the advantages for which I had been hoping ... and more. Putting my gear in the RV took the weight off my bike and made traveling so much easier; that alone made a huge difference in my riding. I also had the benefit of their experience and help with my equipment. They had broken spokes, just as I had, and they were able to help me fix mine temporarily.

We rode through Camp Lejune, not missing the humor of me biking through a marine base wearing my incredibly stylish girl's sunglasses. Humor aside, it was a tremendously windy day—blowing about 20 miles an hour and gusting about 30. It might have taken us forever to get through the base, but fortunately we met up with a friend of the guys and we were able to draft behind a pickup truck! It blocked the wind for us, just like we were following a snow plow through a blizzard. With the wind out of the equation, we were able to cruise over 20mph for 10 miles. It was a piece of cake ... with the help, of course.

We stopped at a bike shop to fix my poor tires and the spokes I kept breaking. The bike shop offered me a greatly discounted rate when they learned what we were doing. As if that wasn't enough—Frank actually paid for the rest of my bike repair. What a blessing! I did see the bikes the guys were riding and decided I wanted to raise money for a touring bike while I was in Florida. Having the right bike would help my trip so much.

It wasn't all fun and games with these guys. They had been going a little further than I had each day—50 to 60 miles. It was a little easier without my gear, so I thought I would be okay. Then one day they decided they wanted to try 100 miles—even with the wind. There were times my legs burned so badly that I just wanted to quit, but they kept pushing me to continue. We actually made 99 miles that day because Byron—the one driving the RV—had found a church building with a facility made just to house travelers. It had mattresses, showers, a washer and dryer—and a well-stocked kitchen. We arrived, cleaned ourselves up, and had a chance to share in the service.

After the service, a 15-year old boy gave me $5. I knew it was a lot of money for him and I let him know I appreciated it greatly. The church fed us hot dogs—a great meal after the hard ride we had done that day. Later, as we hung out in the pole-barn type structure, we were given free rein in the camp kitchen—with the instructions to "eat everything we wanted" ... that was music to my ears. I remember thinking, "This might be what heaven will be like." We had cake, baloney sandwiches, and just about any other food we could think of. I sat down with a waffle bowl and a huge scoop of cookies and cream ice cream. The hard ride seemed to be worth it with the great rewards at the end. I knew this was just a small taste of how I would feel when I reached San Francisco.

Day after day, the guys pushed me harder than I normally would have gone, but it was worth it to have the company. They kept me entertained too. The sight of Frank feeding seagulls on the ferry still makes me laugh. Feeding seagulls is normal—but he fed them from his mouth! This is the same guy who, when he decided he needed a break, just rode his bike off the freeway toward a group of trees and fell onto the grass. It wasn't just Frank that kept me laughing either. After a 92 mile ride, we all collapsed. I was recording a video blog when Byron (who had been in the RV the entire day) pretended to ride up on a bicycle, complaining about how hard the ride was and how he was almost hit by a truck. He bragged that he managed to push through and even made dinner in the process. The loafers he was wearing gave him away though. They were all constant sources of amusement.

Things still weren't perfect–even in the group. We had our struggles. As Byron had alluded, one of the guys was nearly hit by a truck that drifted too close to the edge of the road. In the RV, something in the microwave broke and caused it to run constantly, nuking the loaf of bread we had stored in there into a meteorite. We had to turn off the microwave at the breaker to make it stop. Fortunately nothing deadly or disastrous happened.

Without question, one of the worst things on this leg of the trip happened to my iPhone. The road we were riding had rumble strips—the grooves in the pavement that keep drivers from falling asleep and driving off the road. A friend of mine called them "driving by Braille." They are not nearly as much fun on bicycles and we had to cross them from time to time while dodging debris on the road. I had been using a belt clip zip-tied to my handlebars for my phone, so I could check my GPS as I rode. We had gone about four miles for the day, when I looked down to check my phone. It was gone!

I left the four other guys behind me and rode back to find it. I wondered what the odds of finding an iPhone were when it had randomly fallen at some point of a four mile stretch of road.

The odds are apparently decent; however, the odds of finding an iPhone intact ... somewhat less. I rode back to the guys to give them my report.

"Well?" Joel had asked me.

"Found it," I told him with an incredulous smile. "It had a few scratches, though."

I held out the handful of completely smashed bits. I regretted not bringing a shovel to pick up all the pieces. At least I didn't need it for directions this leg.

But I was left wondering what this meant for my trip. I still determined to not let it get me down. I would learn later, that my reaction was a great testimony to the guys.

I just prayed God would provide what I needed when I needed it. I knew God could answer that prayer; He was still answering them for us every day. At one point, when the wind became brutal, Joel prayed for a wind to be with us. His prayer was answered by a Hurricane ... literally! We were able to draft an RV—a Hurricane model— at about 20mph and get another break from the wind. I had come to love drafting ... but I still kept my hand on the brake ... just in case.

The weather this leg was some of the worst I had encountered. The wind and the rain constantly slowed us. Fortunately, God always provided a way through—or shelter in—the storms. Usually the RV was significantly ahead of us, scouting out a place to stay. We found overpasses to keep us dry. At one point, we even had a stranger stop and let us rest in his truck while the storm passed.

Another day, we had just about every tire in the pack

go flat and we had to hitch a ride to Wal-Mart to pick up six new tubes. Two of those were bad out of their boxes. We lost so much time that we decided to ride through the night—an entirely different experience. We had to focus on the ground directly in front of our bikes so we didn't run over anything detrimental. Just to make it more "exciting" we were traveling through an area marked by "Bear Crossing" signs. As we rode along, a rustling in the forest next to the road startled us all. Mentally preparing to run or pedal away from the roaring and snarling gigantic bear leaping out, we were instead quite relieved to see a few deer.

Arriving at the gas station on the other side of the woods, the man working there looked surprised to see us. There was, he told us, a 600lb bear who frequently roamed the woods we had just navigated. I thanked God for keeping us safe. And again, as difficult as the situation was, I was so grateful to have my new friends to share it.

As if having friends, encouragers, my weight lifted, and even a mobile shower wasn't enough, God continued to bless me with support from people back home. When I was down to $20 again, my mom called and said a church friend put $100 into my account. Ron, my friend in Ohio who owns a dumpster company, also gave me some money. I shared my story with about 10 ladies at a McDonald's playground and one of them gave me $12. A conversation in a gas station earned me $5 for the food I just bought.

Later, we rode through the drive-through line at a McDonald's. The girl in the car behind us made a joke about it, but I just looked at her and said, "God loves you." Almost immediately, she looked like she might cry. She said she had been wrestling with a major decision. She had prayed for a sign - and I had the chance for God to use me as one. In addition, our talk ended with her blessing me with another $20.

I'll confess at this point I spent some of that money on a new pair of sunglasses.

During this leg, we also met Joey's mom and sister at a water park and were let in for free. We had double the benefits: a place to swim and the ability to wash our clothes at the same time.

I also met an interesting character at Burger King. I was filling up my CamelBak—the backpack containing my water, fed through a flexible straw running over my shoulder. While I had it in my hand, a young child walked up to me and asked me if that was for hiking. I was amazed that at such a young age he had no fear. He could talk to anyone and speak his mind. That's how we should be. Somewhere between birth and 18 years old we lose that sense of faith and it is instead replaced by a system of pride and shame. But I have to think God wants us to have no fear.

Without a doubt, the best part of the trip was the final

stretch. As we rolled into Frank's church in Immokalee, FL on June 26th, probably 60 people stood there cheering us towards the finish line. It was beautiful to see all of them waiting for us.

Then I realized they were waiting for *them*. My time with Frank, Adam, Joel, and Joey had come to a close. They had succeeded in their goal—riding 1200 miles and raising money for a great cause. Their friends and family waited for them ... but not for me. My destination still lay across the country—San Francisco with its iconic Golden Gate Bridge. My spirits were uplifted though; I knew a reception like that would await me in the future.

For my temporary respite, Joel invited me to his house for dinner and a movie before I had to continue onward.

I started this leg feeling lonely, despite all the blessings I had been given. It was interesting to think of Adam and Eve. Adam was made first and had everything provided for him. Yet God still looked at Adam and said, "It is not good for man to be alone" (Gen 2:18 NIV). The Christian life—and all life—is played out with one another. Friends supply accountability, challenge, support, and even laughter. We don't always stay with the same friends our whole lives, but they always stay with us. I'll never forget Frank, Adam, Joel, and Joey.

7 RUTYNA ZABICIA

On Monday, June 27th, Joel drove me 45 miles to get a head start on my day. My iPhone was still smashed, but Joel gave me $100 to help towards the replacement; I just had to find a store now.

Still, the farther away from Joey, Adam, Joel, and Frank I rode, the more I seemed to feel alone. I had gotten used to being around people again, and now I had returned to the routine of being alone. My best friend had a saying from his Polish heritage: *Rutyna Zabicia*: Routine Kills. Here I was, back into the same thing I had been experiencing. The only way it could have been worse would have been for it to rain. Sure enough, just like a movie cue: the rain started misting down. The final clincher came as I rolled up to a to a 2-mile long bridge with a large "No Bicycles" sign.

I stopped, feeling my guts drop into my feet, weighing

them down so much I couldn't pedal one more time. I wanted to quit. I thought about how great it would feel to go home and be with my family. I didn't know where those thoughts were coming from, but I couldn't stop them. I figured the bridge was a sign. I had made a good run; I had biked over 2000 miles—quite a feat for someone like me who wasn't a professional biker.

I called my brother Tom. He thought the timing of my call was strange: he had a dream the previous night that I surprised him on his porch. Normally Tom had been a great source of encouragement on the trip, but this time he unknowingly made me feel homesick. He was telling me about all the fun he was having at home. My parents owned a house in the country that sat on a beautiful piece of land with a three acre pond on it. Tom told me about a party they had; it made me miss all the fun times from the past. In my mind, I pictured myself turning around, heading north, and going home to enjoy the summer with them. I knew if I kept on my current trip it would be close to winter when I wrapped up my trip and there would be no swimming for me this year.

After I told Tom about how I was thinking about quitting, we prayed someone in a truck would come and pick me up and haul me across the bridge. He even went as far to pray for a red truck. As soon as we hung up, I started looking for it. No trucks came the first minute … the first five minutes … the first 10 minutes. I finally had to face reality and make a decision. I knew God could send a truck if He wanted to, but maybe this was a test for me.

I thought about how far God had already brought me. It had seemed like only a day had passed since I left my church in Johnstown. I realized it would probably seem the same way when I reached San Francisco. I would be so much happier if I could reach my goal and then praise God that I never quit. I knew it would be nice to stop, go back to my family, and swim, but that was a bad exchange. The glory of undertaking such a difficult journey would far overshadow a temporary pleasure. That joy would make all the trials seem like an overnight trip.

Suddenly I felt a blast of courage and motivation to continue the trip, like the Holy Spirit drove me forward. I decided I was going to ignore the signs and ride. As I started across the bridge, I realized there was no median—just a one-foot wide concrete step to hold the railing in place. On the other side of the rail, a 40-foot drop waited. Trying to keep to the side of the bridge and out of traffic that close to a drop, while balancing a bicycle with 75 lbs of gear on the back, inspired instant and heart-felt prayer.

I kept God on my mind and before I knew it, I suddenly passed the leg of the trip that almost sent me home. God is always good.

After the bridge, I continued to the closest mall. But

there was no Apple store there. The closest was Ft. Myers - where I had just left there. The next one was another 100 miles ahead in Tampa. I felt crushed again; I expected things to be easier after overcoming the despair at the bridge. But here despair was again, sitting in my behind like a lead weight. In fact, I just plopped down on the curb and let the feeling permeate my behind. That's when a security guard pulled up to where I was sitting.

I thought for a moment, Maybe God sent him to help me.

"Stand up. There's no sitting allowed on the curbs," he said and then drove away.

Nice touch, I thought, feeling my despair turn into anger. *What else could go wrong?*

The answer: "a flat tire."

This was as low as I had felt. I decided just to give up for the day and find some place to camp. I called church after church—and no one would have me. Finally, I found a Lutheran church and, even though no one was there, I just camped for the night.

I hit the road the next day still feeling down, but determined to at least make it to my aunt's house in Clearwater, FL. On the way, I was finally able to pick up an iPhone that had only one piece rather than a couple hundred. Even that was a blessing. A new phone would have cost me $650; If I could have waited until my upgrade time, it would have been $200, but I could not wait. I explained to the clerk at the store what I was doing - as well as the gravity of not having a phone. He understood and we were able to work out a deal for a replacement.

Even the $200 stung a bit. Plus I was frustrated since I had lost all the pictures from my original phone. Thankfully, I had uploaded some of my videos to YouTube and they were still safe.

With the hole in my wallet and a permeating feeling of despair, I arrived at my Aunt Robin's, knowing I was in desperate need of a break from my depression. Sometimes it takes a deep theological paradigm to fix an ailing heart.

Sometimes it takes a simple pleasure. Aunt Robin's house was fully stocked with Dr. Pepper and Fruity Pebbles. Fully stocked, by the way, meant about 15 cases stacked in her kitchen. I knew we had to be related

"How long will that last you?" I asked her.

"About a week and a half," she said.

She wasn't joking. She drank about five of them every day. Still, the rest at Robin's house was a nice break. I actually still was able to swim—this time in beautiful warm water. I had forgotten about that when I was feeling low earlier. If I had gone home I would have missed out on some amazing swimming in the Gulf of Mexico. Robin kept me fed and rested. On the fourth of July, we watched fireworks.

I visited a bike store and found I could upgrade my rear rim for only $220. That would help me out immensely in preventing the flat tires I had been experiencing. Now, I just needed the $220. Of course, God provided whenever I had a need, so I prayed He would somehow give me the money for a new rim. Sure enough, money started coming out of nowhere. A friend of my mom's gave me $100. Tom put $20 into my account. Robin gave me another $20. I even visited First Christian Church in Howard Park Beach, FL, and had 7 elderly people give me $13. Robin bought an iPhone case and screen protector—a huge blessing. It was $70, but the peace of mind was priceless; I didn't want my new phone falling off my bike. Even with all of this, though, I was still about $30 short of the $220 I needed for my new wheel. I figured God must have had some other idea in mind. I went back to the bike store, bought some more water bottles, and had some maintenance done. I also grabbed plenty of tubes, as I figured I would still be changing them quite often.

While I was resting at Aunt Robin's, I watched a video with Francis Chan about people across the globe who were literally starving. It shocked me to see how many people didn't have enough to eat daily. I had known hunger on this trip—but it was nothing compared to the global statistics. In fact, I did the calculation and figured out that in just the time I had been filming videos for my ride, 5642 people had died of starvation. I really wanted the new bike tire, but I could hardly justify the purchase seeing what I had just seen.

I had a little over $190 at this point. The video I watched convicted me so much I thought about donating that to the cause. In the Bible, Jesus praised a widow who gave a pittance of an offering out of her poverty, rather than the wealthy who were showing off and giving huge amounts of money (Luke 21). I thought about how a widow gave Elijah the last of her food and God blessed her with more oil than she knew what to do with (I Kings 17). The thought scared me—I could use the money, if not for the bike repairs, certainly for food and supplies.

But I had a feeling God would take care of me. So I donated $180 to Food for the Hungry (www.fh.org). I determined when I got back home I would look into churches that did food packing and would help them out. I did some quick research, and the statistics shocked me. When I was home and working, it was nothing for me to go out and spend $8 to $10 on Chipotle for lunch—one meal! Here on the road, I could easily use that to eat for a day ... or two. I could probably stretch that into three or four if I had to. Then I learned that in some countries, $8 could buy 32 meals.

Waking up the next morning with only $13 left was certainly a test. As I left to continue my journey, I said goodbye to my aunt and started walking out the door.

Robin handed me $100. It didn't even take God eight hours to replenish my funds. How much more glorious could God be? He never hesitated to take care of me— even though I never did anything to deserve it other than being his child. I felt immediate joy fill my steps.

Donating that money was an interesting step in my faith journey. I didn't give out of guilt or obligation. I gave because I love people—even the ones I've never met. I think Christianity can sometimes come off as condemning. When Tom and Ron used to preach to me, all I heard was "You're living the wrong way, Mikey. You're a bad person." They certainly weren't saying it that blatantly, but that's definitely the way I felt. I wanted nothing to do with that kind of Christianity. I knew I sinned and did bad things, but there were a whole lot of people who did worse things than I did. I thought my life was good enough.

It wasn't until Tom's comment about "God is love" that things started falling into perspective. All of their preaching suddenly started making sense. I stopped looking at Christianity as a way of wanting less sin, and instead starting wanting more of God. I remembered a saying that "the greatest wisdom is knowing that you know nothing." People can't learn if they think they know everything. Once we realize that, we open ourselves up to the whole learning process.

For instance, one of the biggest arguments against

Christianity is, "Why doesn't God just show up and fix everything?" The answer is simple: we don't know. We don't understand it and we probably never will. For instance, why are there people starving in the world? Why doesn't God make food magically appear in front of them? Yet, I see resources all around me. The money I gave was relatively small compared to the need, but I wondered what would happen if everyone who could afford it gave $180. We could put a huge dent in the hunger problem. Going back to my theological thinking, it's not that God won't solve our problems, it's almost like He's looking to us to do it so we can learn and grow. He's given us the resources; we just need to release them.

We also see statements in the Bible that in order to understand, we have to believe first. Why? Because God said it! We also have a lot of people who try to study the Bible cover-to-cover—and that's a great thing—but they fail to realize the two most basic truths. We are supposed to love God and love our neighbors (Luke 10:27). If we can manage those two things, then everything else falls into place. I cannot sin if I'm remembering to love God and love my fellow human being.

8 THE DARK SIDE OF HUMANITY

Along my travels, I found a car back in the woods. I joked on my video blog that it was a "little bit of a fixer-upper." It had probably sat back in the woods for 20 years. It was just a shell that looked as if it had caught fire before rusting completely through. I think God sees us the same way I saw the car. This thing had no value to the world at all. Yet someone, with the right tools, talent, and time, could have made it look like new.

That's the way I had been seeing the church lately. It has some problems, but it has so much potential too. I wanted to find a group of people who could see the church for what it could be—people who wanted to start out by meeting together and confessing their doubt, pride, and shame. I would love to be a part of a group of people who can admit we do not deserve the glory of God, but understand Christ has made that possible. From that mindset, we are so well-equipped to love God and worship Him. We can praise God for our breath, heartbeat, the earth we walk on.

I had an idea on this trip. Well, Conrad and I actually worked on this one together, but I had a lot of time to think about it while I was on the road. I want to start a foundation—a foundation built out of gold, so to speak. I want to build a system where a group of people can come together and are so filled with the Holy Spirit that they cannot walk into the room without shining. People will be attracted from miles away—and it blows away any existing notion of church. It will make the current church seem that it's not even close to being holy. It sounds crazy—and we may be crazy, but the great thing about Christianity and God is that we are supposed to be crazy. Jesus was considered "crazy" in His day. He did miracles, healings, and teaching—and they were all crazy.

We need something different. The current routine is not working: *Rutyna Zabicia.* The world is still at work and the devil stills seems to be in charge every day. This movement I'm thinking about, these people assemble every day, filled with the Holy Spirit—not to show off, but with the purpose of coming together and solving each other's problems. I want us to actually act like the body of Christ is one in unity—just like it is supposed to be. This isn't happening now. I want people to want to come together—to feel shameless enough to let others know their problems and let each other solve them. If someone needs a roof fixed, the church should be able to assemble and fix it. If someone's rent needs paid, the community can get together and help.

I know my ideas aren't new; I'm sure many people have thought about doing it. Even I had been thinking about these ideas long before my trip. At the time, I had been working for my oldest brother Phil - known as Phil Jr., to differentiate him from my father - finishing basements. Even though Phil ran a great business, I couldn't say the same about many of the other companies I saw. As I listened to other people's stories, I became tired of the way the world worked. I hated seeing companies scamming people with all their greed. I would ask myself, "Why do people let the things of this world get them down? Why do people get so stressed out about bills and work? Why does everyone live so selfishly?"

There was too much evil in this world and I felt like I needed to at least try to help fix it. I started to do my own handyman work for donations only, thinking I could spread some love that way, but it wasn't enough for me. I remember helping out a friend who had a bathroom leak in her condo. The repair wasn't much, but the condo association and her renter's insurance couldn't agree on who should pay the pay the bill. It seemed silly to me that someone who paid their dues as long as she had, couldn't get the least bit of help when she needed it.

After helping her, I knew I wanted to do more. I wanted to help everyone I could. I wanted people to know "God is Love" and there needed to be more of it going around. I thought about traveling the country doing construction work—remodeling bathrooms and working as a general handyman. In order to do that though, I was going to need to be free from anything that would encumber me.

By Sunday, July 10th, I was part way there. I had left my Aunt Robin's house and landed in Orlando, FL where I stayed with my brother Guy in his hotel room. I enjoyed all the amenities I could during this rest time. I even had a chance to see my sister-in-law and nephew when they came down to stay. Being able to travel with new friends was great, but nothing compared to spending time with my family. At the same time, I knew this would be the last

 time I'd see familiar faces until I finally finished this trip and reunited with my family.

Mike's sister-in-law Donya, Mike, and her son Brooks take time to pose for a picture in Orlando

Mike's bother Guy, Guy's son Brooks, and Mike.

Unfortunately, even in the midst of such amazing friendship, I still saw reminders of how bad this world could be. As I drove around Orlando with Guy, we saw all sorts of evidences of people caught in their own *Rutyna Zabicia.*

As always, God spoke to me even in these dire circumstances. I had no doubt about God's goodness. Yet, the world was a terrible place at times. How could a good God create all this?

One of the first things I noticed was that not everything that we call "evil" is the same. Some of it is natural—having to bike through rain, the construction staple that flattened my tire, even the gnats I had to bike through. I didn't think God actually caused any of those things to happen—they were just all part of life. Rain happens. It's not all bad; it certainly has its benefits. Just because it was uncomfortable for me didn't mean some farmer close by didn't need it. The staple was just "there." Things fall apart and decay; it's a natural part of life. The gnats: well, riding through a swarm of bugs that die on contact is hardly painful or detrimental ... it's just gross.

There are also evils of choice. When Guy and I were driving around Cocoa Beach, we found a "gentlemen's" club. The business alone is such a misnomer. I have a hard time calling someone who views that sort of entertainment a "gentleman." To make it worse, the name of the club was "Cheaters." The name clearly showed the intent of the club; it advocated not being faithful to one's wife. As a single guy, I certainly was not an expert on love, yet I still knew a fundamental truth from my short time as a Christian: God shows us love must be an action. It's a choice. God loved me when I was an unlovable goon speeding through Los Angeles. God loved me when I thought a casual relationship and just being vaguely aware of His existence with Him was perfectly fine. He loved me, not because of what I do, but because of who I am—His child. When I find the right person, I want to be in a position where I choose to love her and choose to show her that type of love every day—not running off to some club to pay for a cheap substitute.

There seemed to be one other kind of evil evident

from my time in Orlando. Some philosophers call it "maximum evil" or "evil against innocents." We had the chance to drive by and see some of the sights connected with the Casey Anthony trial. In July of 2008 Casey's two-year old daughter Caylee went missing. Her body was found in December of that same year. Because Casey provided false evidence, she was charged with her daughter's murder. She was acquitted.

Guy and I drove by and saw the memorial to Caylee. Stuffed animals, toys, and cards sat piled around it. My heart felt heavy as we drove past the sight. In the grand scheme of things, it really didn't matter who did it. Nothing would bring back a sweet two-year old who had done nothing wrong to the human race. She wasn't being punished; she was a victim. Whoever killed her was the evil one—the one who chose to take another human life not even capable of defending itself.

I took this trip to build my faith, but more and more I just saw how bad humankind can be. It broke my heart. I knew God made us in His image to do good things, but we just kept messing that up. I guess I was starting to understand life from God's perspective a bit more. I could see He loves us unconditionally; but sometimes I had to question why he does. In fact, if I saw the things I did and had the power to change things, I might be tempted to obliterate the entire human race. Yet, He's so patient and wants us to learn from our mistakes so we'll come back to Him.

It brought me to a stunning realization, going back to Tom's statement. "God is love." God loved us so much that He created humankind with free will. Some human beings choose to abuse their freewill and do bad things with it, but others do remarkably wonderful things with it. It's the only way love works.

Fortunately we know from the Bible He will set things right eventually. Until that happens, He doesn't allow us to suffer alone. When I thought about how I'm not sure of where my food and meals will come from, I realized Jesus lived the same way. When I thought about friends I lost and friends I had to leave—so did He. And most of all, I realized no matter how much I suffered, it paled in comparison with the suffering He underwent on the cross. He laid down His life for each and every one of us, so we would be able to come back to God. That's what makes Christianity different. Every religion and every worldview has to explain why evil exists. But only in Christianity does God suffer with us. It was a humbling thought to say the least.

9 TRIALS AND TEMPTATIONS

On the 12th of July, I decided to put Florida behind me. I headed towards Leesburg, FL, calling churches along the way. I was turned down by quite a few, but eventually found Faith Community Church, Pastor Kevin, and his youth minister Matt. I knew that would be a good place as soon as I walked in and saw the youth duct taping each other to the walls. Pastor Kevin gave me a chance to tell my testimony in front of the small group of teens. It was an incredible experience! Not too long before I had been sitting in the front of Tom's truck listening to his testimony, and there I was talking about my own faith. Before I went up to talk to them, I felt the nerves bunch up in my stomach. I wasn't sure what I was going to say. I was a baby Christian and really didn't have all the answers. I remembered what Jesus said to his disciples, "When they arrest you and hand you over, do not worry beforehand about what you are to say, but say whatever is given you in that hour; for it is not you who speak, but it is the Holy Spirit." (Mark 13:11 NIV). It hit me that I wasn't an expert in Christianity, but I didn't have to be one. I just had to talk about what I knew. The session went great. I just shared all about my trip and the ways I had seen God work.

After I shared my story, the youth gave me some of their leftover pizza. I felt like I was getting back into the swing of things. Even better, I called ahead to my next stop, Chiefland Church of God, and talked to youth leader, Gene, and found a place to stay there.

The next day, on the way to Chiefland, I was cruising on the sidewalk about 13 mph, happily singing along to my music. Then I learned that, as wonderful as the high points are, life can be fleeting at times. I approached an intersection where the traffic moving the same direction as me had the green light. Figuring it was safe to cross, I proceeded like I was going to bike across the street. About six feet from the crossroad, I caught a truck out of the corner of my eye, going too fast for an intersection like this, as it turned directly in front of me. I braced myself for the impact, locking up both tires and sliding my bike sideways towards the Toyota Tundra. I stiff-armed the black door panel with my left hand—becoming painfully aware of how an NFL quarterback feels attempting to hold off a linebacker. The bike and I scraped down the whole side of the truck.

The good news was that, as terrifying as the whole experience was, it could certainly have been a lot worse. Nothing happened to either me or my bike, and the truck suffered a small scuff. Praise the Lord! It did shock me to see how quickly my fortunes could change. It would have been too easy for a situation like that to turn out badly. It was also a further reminder I needed to be careful of cyclists when I was back and driving my car again.

I collected myself and continued onward, trusting God for my safety—and saying an extra prayer just in case. About 30 miles before Chiefland Church of God, I stopped at a gas station for snacks and rest. A driver delivering snacks for Frito Lay walked into the store.

He looked at me for a moment and then asked, "Are you Mike?"

I was shocked that a stranger knew my name. He turned out to be Gene from the church where I was heading! Chance meetings like that always amazed me.

And as always, the good and the bad come together. I arrived at Gene's church and took some time out to read from the book of James, "Consider it pure joy, my brothers and sisters, whenever you face trials of many kinds, because you know that the testing of your faith produces perseverance." It was a wonderfully encouraging passage … in theory. When my tent pole snapped in my hand, it was a little more difficult to swallow, but I knew I had to "consider it pure joy." Trials come into all Christian's lives at some point. And mine continued at 6:30 the next morning. A truck pulled up and the man who lived on the church property asked if I had permission to stay. Even though I told him Gene had given me permission, he still didn't believe me—and he certainly wasn't pleasant about it. I really wanted to question him about Luke 10:27 "Love the Lord your God with all your heart and with all your soul and with all your strength and with all your mind'; and, 'Love your neighbor as yourself" (NIV). Nevertheless, I continued down the road determined to make the most of the day.

I ended up "making the most of the day" at a gas station while the rain poured. Two bikers—as in motorcyclists—from Memphis joined me. I had a chance to tell them my story.

They told me, "There's no better reason to do what you're doing than for Christ." One of them gave me $50; the other one gave me $20. There were certainly blessings in midst of the trials I was facing.

I took advantage of the break to call churches in Tallahassee. Out of the 15 churches I called, only two of them actually answered. One said they didn't have grass, but did have a facility with showers and a room to stay in. However, the person who told me about this said they had to call "Steve" to get permission. When they called back, apparently "Steve" said "no" since the interns were out of town and no one else was there.

The second church had to check with someone as well, but no one ever returned my call. This became too commonplace during my trip. One church told me they "were sure I'd find a place." He recognized the need, but didn't want to be the one to fill it. It reminded me of what James wrote to the early church: "If one of you says to them, 'Go in peace; keep warm and well fed,' but does nothing about their physical needs, what good is it? In the same way, faith by itself, if it is not accompanied by action, is dead" (James 2:16–17 NIV). It broke my heart to be treated this way by the church. I just camped on the side of the road. It wasn't the end of the world for me. And unfortunately it wouldn't be the last church to treat me that way.

I started to think churches were not the place I wanted to look for love. As I looked back at my trip, I'd been blessed more outside of churches than I had inside. I decided to go back to asking strangers for hospitality. It was a bittersweet decision to say the least. I thought the church should be better than this.

I pondered more about my salvation. It was one thing to make a decision to become a Christian, but an entirely different one to try to walk that out each day. Those trials and tribulations James talked about to the early church are still with us today.

Temptation is a huge obstacle to Christianity. Part of

the challenge of walking as a Christian is getting rid of sin. The best thing to do is remove oneself from that situation. I thought I had done that when I started this trip. I knew a lot of the thoughts I struggled with came from the television—and there was certainly a lack of that here. I thought about when I had stayed at the beach a couple weeks earlier. Lindsay, one of the other campers there, had invited me to party with her and her friends, I felt something in me say it might be a mistake to go, so I had stayed behind and read my Bible instead. I was reminded of Joseph in the Bible, when Potiphar's wife was hitting on him; he ran away and got himself out of the temptation to sleep with his boss's wife. It seems a huge key to avoiding temptation is asking God to help. I Peter 1:7 says, "Submit yourselves, then, to God. Resist the devil, and he will flee from you" (NIV).

Trials are another difficulty on the Christian walk. Something as simple as a gnat flying into my eye proved to be a trial. I tried for 20 minutes to get the little guy out and he wouldn't budge. I prayed and pulled into a gas station about 10 minutes later and he worked his way out.

Weather also seemed to be a perpetual trial. I learned quickly on this trip that I had two choices to keep my clothes clean. One consisted of using a washer and dryer if I had the facilities available. It was during one such stop that I learned my iPod was not waterproof. After trying so hard to keep my electronics dry, I just threw one into the washer (via the pocket in my shorts).

The other way of doing laundry involved taking a shower with my clothes so we all got clean at the same time. Unfortunately my way lacked a good dryer, so normally I hung my clothes out to dry. That worked great ... unless it was raining. Since I was already as wet as I could be, I biked onward. I wondered what could make it worse.

Mud.

Finding my way onto an unpaved road, I had to walk my bike six miles to the Georgia border through soaking, clinging, slippery mud. I found a paved road for about ten miles until it turned into another mud path. I fought my way through dirt, mud, and ruts.

Mike's bike, the wheels caked with mud from his trek.

Down to my last $3, I called Conrad and had him pray. I also talked to him about my new church idea and we brought Tom in on a three way call. I questioned if the modern church is really living by scripture.

Matthew 7 talks about two men who built houses. One built it on a stone foundation; the other built it on the sand. When trials came—which they always do—the sandy one was destroyed, but the one on the rock stood firm. Jesus said those who built their houses on the rock are those who hear His words AND put them into practice. I wanted our church to be that way. We decided to tell each other our needs. For one of the first times this trip, I had to confess I was out of money. It was difficult for me to say, but I realized if I wanted this new church to help each other with their needs, it had to start with us. Tom went to my bank right then and deposited $40 so I could eat. Conrad put in $50 as well. Praise God! I also was able to help Tom and Conrad with their burdens. Since theirs were more spiritual in nature, I could actually help them ... by praying for them. I thought to myself that this is the kind of stuff we should be doing daily!

After the conversation, I felt my spirits lift again! I was back to feeling invincible. It showed me why we need to be in God's presence daily. That's the most important lesson I've learned on this trip: we have to constantly keep God on our minds. And we should keep our electronics out of the washer.

When I encountered those trials I had to force myself to look at the positive side of every situation—talking to God about it all the while. They are difficult, but Paul says, "We know that in all things God works for the good of those who love him, who have been called according to his purpose" (Romans 8:28, NIV). When Christians can take hold of that verse, it's life changing. It brings confidence and joy. I'd never have made it through this trip if I worried about where I would stay, if a car might hit me, what I would eat, if I would face wild animals, etc. Instead, I enjoyed the ride and looked forward each day to what God had in store for me.

The best part of the trials, though, was that they made the blessings seem so much better. I stopped for lunch at Wendy's and ordered three chicken sandwiches and a small fry. I really wanted a Frosty, but I couldn't justify a "want" with my money situation. It turned out my food took too long to make, so Wendy's offered me a Frosty and an upsized fry for free. Jesus rocks!

Later I rode to Burger King. I didn't feel right just taking their water, so I ordered a small Dr. Pepper—which they gave free to me anyway. While I was filling up my CamelBak, a lady pointed at the sign on my back that said *Bike For Christ* and said, "That's cool." She shared her testimony with me. She had spent time in prison, had gotten saved there, and now did evangelistic work—back in the prisons. While we were talking, a family walked up to us said, "We love Jesus, too." As Audrey started sharing, she told me her son Jesse was a gospel singer. Since we were the only people in the restaurant, we asked the manager if it was okay to hear him sing. Jesse got his guitar and gave us an impromptu concert right there in Burger King. He sat in his t-shirt and plaid shorts, surrounded by fast food tables, and belted out a beautiful version of "Your Grace is Enough." The words touched me deeply, realizing I was doing this whole trip on God's grace. Afterwards, we exchanged numbers. They lived about 2 days ride away and said I was welcome to stay with them when I got there.

This leg of my journey ended where it began, though—in great tribulation. I found out fast that the road I needed to take the whole way was nothing short of a disaster area. It was by far the most difficult and most dangerous road I travelled—a popular log trucker route with no shoulder and there were no alternative routes. It felt like the bridge all over again, but this time it was 80 miles of danger. Still, I prayed and continued down it, finding myself constantly moving off the road to allow trucks and cars to pass. I stopped at a peach stand. The worker told me another biker came through and blogged on his site that this road was the most dangerous road he'd been on. On the bright side, he gave me 2 free peaches, a Gatorade, and he filled up my water.

After about 40 miles, I pulled into a rest stop. With the

delays from dodging traffic, it was starting to get dark—and that was one extra challenge I wasn't ready to throw into the mix. At first, I thought of hitching a ride through the troublesome area. I prayed God would send me the right truck to get me to my destination. I don't think I saw a single truck pull into the rest stop after that. As much as it hurt to do so, I decided to call it quits for the night. It was dangerous enough during the day and I didn't want to test God's protection too much. The security guards, thankfully, said I could camp at the rest area. And better yet, I had the chance to share my testimony with them. We had a great conversation.

As I turned in for the evening, my thoughts turned towards the day ahead. The road ran another 50 miles to Tuscaloosa. I took a strange comfort in Jesus's words, "Therefore do not worry about tomorrow, for tomorrow will worry about itself. Each day has enough trouble of its own" (Matthew 6:34 NIV)

10 THE BIG BIKE BLESSING

On Sunday, July 24th, I headed towards Holly Springs, MS. I experienced much of the same challenges and blessings as the previous legs of the trip. Several churches declined my requests to stay until one finally accepted me. I had the chance to share my story in front of 30 people. Again, I became so aware of my shortcomings as a public speaker. But just like my biking, the more I did it, the more I got used to it. My nervousness diminished quickly as I just shared my heart with that group.

The next day I headed towards Memphis to meet a man named Hugh—a friend of my grandfather's. I had a great unexpected blessing on the way as someone stopped and filled up my water bottles for me. Once I arrived in Memphis, Hugh let me stay in his guest bedroom, and use his shower. He even took me to Steak and Shake for dinner. The next day he drove me 30 miles to the other side of the Mississippi. He not only saved me from another long and treacherous trip across a bridge, but it also gave me a chance to sit back and gaze out the car window at the mighty river. I realized I was crossing over to the other side of the United States.

I picked a nearby city and continued on my journey, calling the Church of Christ there along the way. No one answered, but while I waited, I had the chance to meet Terri and Charles—a pair of hitchhikers on their way home from Texas. As I shared my story with them, I learned they were both Christians, but ones who had a difficult life. I prayed for them, somewhat sad that I couldn't help them out more. They were a reminder of how many hurting people there are in the world. As much as I felt isolated on my trip, I knew there was more I would have to do when I finished. There were more "Terri and Charles's" around and they needed help—a listening ear, an encouraging word, or a caring hand.

After they went along their way, I tried calling the church again. This time they answered and welcomed me to stay. When I arrived, I saw they were doing a Vacation Bible School. They let me sit in the service and later on I ate with them. Afterwards, James from the church took me to a hotel and paid for the room! A room is better than a tent anytime! Praise the Lord! I enjoyed the room, shower, and air conditioning. I thanked God aloud for the blessing.

I have no clue how God manages all the decisions we do make—let alone all the ones we could make … and the ones we don't make. After a short, 21-mile ride to Searcy, AR. I found myself passing a McDonald's and having to make a conscious decision to stop or continue onward. It seemed to take forever to make the choice. I had already eaten, but I could have used the rest, the recharge, and a refill for my water. The decision to stop and do that would forever alter my trip, my understanding of God, and the amount of good one person can do.

In McDonald's, a stranger approached me—and surprised me at first. He introduced himself as Brian and asked if I was planning on eating. He offered to pay for whatever I wanted. Praise the Lord. I had actually just eaten so I just ordered a fruit smoothie. Brian and his friend John invited me to join them. I did, and I told them my story. It turned out Brian was a youth minister and John was his intern. He asked me what my plans were and where I was staying for the night. I told him the truth: I had only ridden 21 miles, but this whole trip was based around the idea that I had no plans.

"God makes my plans," I said.

That must have been the right answer. Brian and John both said I could stay with them. First, though, they

took me to a bike shop so I could get a bike check up.
That changed everything. I fell in love as soon as I walked
in the door. I felt my breath catch. My eyes fixed straight
ahead; I couldn't move if I wanted. That was one of the
most surreal experiences of the trip. It was … the most
amazing bike: a Jamis Aurora elite, top of the line, $1600
touring bicycle. It had been ridden for about 100 miles
and the store was selling it for $1290 … still way out of my
league, but it would have been a sweet ride.

I had a fleeting thought. If the shop was selling a
used bike, they might want to buy mine too. I asked and
they said they would buy my bike, but only for $275. I
couldn't believe my $900 bike was already worth less than
a third of what I paid for it. To make matters worse, the
bike appraisal gave me confirmation that my bike was
indeed falling apart. The gears were worn. The chain was
about to break. The guy at the shop told me that without
maintenance soon, I was going to have some major
issues. That was not the news I wanted to hear halfway
across the country.

I hurt deeply. I was frustrated at the guy who sold
me the bike. I felt defeated knowing it might not even last
the trip. I was irritated I didn't have over $1000 to buy a
new bike. As I felt myself spinning out of control, I
stopped, took a deep breath, and prayed. I knew God had
to have something amazing in store for me.

Later that day, Brian and John invited me to a youth

camp to share my story in front of 60–70 teens. I had virtually no time to prepare for a talk in front of the largest audience I had ever addressed. As we sang worship songs and drew closer to the moment I'd have to step on the stage, I felt the butterflies well up in my stomach.

"God, this is all for you," I prayed quietly. "I'm giving you everything. I want Your words to come out of my mouth; this is for Your glory and not mine."

Brian introduced me. I spoke for about 15 minutes and answered around 20 questions for them. It all seemed pretty low key until after I finished. Suddenly, teenagers bombarded me—asking me to sign their t-shirts. A couple of people even handed me cash to help my trip. At first it started to go to my head, but I realized that—once again—it wasn't about me. It was all about God's glory.

It was an amazing experience ... and it didn't stop there. After that, Brian and John took me to their church and I spoke again—this time for about 40 different teens and their parents. I had more questions and more money handed to me. Then a few of us went to Snow Island—a snow cone store. I met a bunch of great people, two of whom handed me $100 each. The generosity of the people I met on this stop floored me. I was so glad I decided to be on God's schedule and not my own.

Breakfast with John, Brian, and Brian's son Lincoln started the next day. I had planned to join them on a trip to the lake with the teenagers, camp up there, and continue on my way. It would knock about 20 miles off my trip and provide some fun along the way. Those were my plans.

God had better ones.

While about 15 people loaded up in the church bus, I waited outside with my bike. John, Brian, and Angela—a parent of one of the kids in the youth group—talked together for a bit, they got off the bus and Angela told me she and her husband Chris wanted to help me with my bike situation. But they didn't want me to get any bike— they were going to help me get the bike I had seen in the shop ... my dream bike. Quite a few people from the church chipped in, and Angela and Chris made up the difference.

I was in shock.

I wanted to rush over to the bike shop immediately, but we had our trip to the lake. Suddenly the best thing I had planned for the day paled in comparison to what God had in store for me. I called the bike shop and asked them to hold the bike ... my bike. Thank God our trip was as much fun as it was, otherwise I might never have gotten my mind off the bike. We did some cliff jumping—30 feet straight down into refreshing water. Of course we also swam. It was great doing normal things again—especially being in the company of other believers.

After the trip, I took my bike in and had them switch

over all of my gear. I picked out a new pump and cleats for my shoes, planning on paying for them on my own. Angela and Chris took care of those too.

With my new gear and my new bike, I felt on top of the world as I walked out of the store. My whole trip seemed to be mine for the conquering. I hugged Angela, feeling it to be a wholly inadequate "Thank You." This bike was amazing. It had disc brakes, lower gears for hill climbing, a steel frame, bigger tires, and even mud guards. It had everything I needed for my trip and more. I ended up staying another night at John's. He bought me dinner. That night I wrote Chris and Angela a message on Facebook thanking them. I was truly amazed.

This bike completely changed my trip. I would be able to put in more miles each day. Plus, I had no way of knowing it at the time, but the next half of my journey would make the first half seem like a cake walk. I'd be up against hills, mountains, wind, and many other obstacles I hadn't encountered yet. This new bike would help me through them.

I had received many blessings on this trip so far and they were all crucial to my trip: food, water, lodging, companionship, bike repairs, and more. Still I had to wonder: what possessed a complete stranger to pay $1000 for another complete stranger to have a bike just to ride away the next day.

In the secular economy, this makes no sense at all.

Businesses use a term called ROI—return on investment. Ideally they want to get more value back from what they put into it. I couldn't give Chris and Angela any kind of return on their investment. I had no money and no job. I wasn't staying put in the community. And yet, here I was—looking at a brand new to me bicycle.

The only way it makes sense is in God's economy, where a couple principles worked together. First, people are most important to God. We should always be investing in people—not things. Jesus told his disciples, "Do not store up for yourselves treasures on earth, where moths and vermin destroy, and where thieves break in and steal. But store up for yourselves treasures in heaven, where moths and vermin do not destroy, and where thieves do not break in and steal. For where your treasure is, there your heart will be also" (Matthew 6:19–21 NIV). The worldly things will all decay and rust—yes that included my bike. But Chris and Angela didn't invest in a bike; they invested in me, and in my trip.

The second part of God's economy sees God as the great "equalizer." Sometimes the financial equation doesn't make sense from a worldly standard. Jesus, in the Sermon on the Mount, tells his disciples some tough statements. He wants them to love their enemies, pray for their persecutors, and give without expecting anything in return (Luke 6:27–36). The idea is that human beings do not sustain Christians; God does—though often through human beings who are willing to give. That's why the principle of "loving God and loving your neighbor" is so important. A few weeks later I would get a message from Chris. He would tell me he had received an unexpected bonus at work ... almost exactly what he paid for the bike! God is so good!

It was amazing to look back and see this all came from a simple decision to walk into a McDonald's at just the right time. Only in God's economy can something like this work. God is so good. Praise Him!

Lowe family at Gander Brook Christian Camp, summer 2012. Left to Right: Chris, Jenna (15), Bradley (11), Anna (17), Caleb (15), Kendall (19), Angela, Carter (21)

11 VIGNETTE: CHRIS AND ANGELA LOWE, SEARCY, AR

Chris and Angela Lowe, as they put it, "don't do things normally" at their house. They are a close-knit family. Chris works for IBM from his home. He is married to Angela and together they have six children, ranging in age from 21 to 11, all of whom they have home-schooled. Their classroom can be in their home in Arkansas, working and participating in a two week long Bible camp, or serving impoverished people in the hills of the Dominican Republic. "We're pointing our children to a life of service in God, not teaching them to serve themselves," Chris said.

Their encounter with Mike Baker was one more step towards that goal. Chris first met Mike at their Wednesday night service. With six kids involved in the youth group, Chris and Angela naturally gravitated toward being involved in their children's lives. Chris was impressed that Mike, a young man with so little public speaking experience prior to his arrival in Searcy, did so well.

However, more than just his speaking abilities impressed Chris.

"I was fascinated and impressed with Mike," Chris said. "I was motivated by him stepping out in faith." Chris admired Mike for the way he put his trust in God for his safety, places to stay, and things to eat.

Even the circumstances of connecting Mike with the church seemed to be God-ordained. The church's youth pastor, Brian, saw Mike at a McDonalds. Which, Chris said, was funny in itself; Brian doesn't even like McDonalds and Mike had already eaten. Yet, they connected and Mike ended up speaking at a camp that day and two church groups that evening.

It was at one of the later meetings that Chris heard Mike talk about his bike. He had it up with him at the front of the class and mentioned that it was the wrong bike. Chris knew he still had quite a ways to go on "that racing bike"; that started him thinking about

Mike's situation.

Later that evening, people in the church went out to a local snow cone place. On the way over, Chris continued thinking about Mike's bike as well as his talk. Mike's example motivated Chris to want to do something. He still didn't say anything, but questioned Mike more about that bike. Later, Chris prayed about what he should do. The next day, as the youth were assembling for a trip to a large lake about 45 minutes north of them, Chris called Angela and had her ask Mike if he would let them buy his bike.

The cost wasn't the prohibitive point. Chris said his job made it so that buying the bike wasn't unreasonable financially. But there was something more to it. Chris didn't want to just throw money at the problem. He wanted to step out in faith the way Mike had done. Providing the funds for the bike became a story in itself. "I told God, 'I don't want to work to pay for this. I don't want to borrow money for it. God, I want you to pay for this bike.'" Chris put the bike on his American Express card, which gave him 30 days to pay the balance in full. Just before the balance came due, Chris received his pay statement from work … with an additional $1200 on it! The extra money had come from a project on which he had worked. He had no clue at the time that there would be a payout to him, but still it arrived just in time.

Chris was glad to be able to help Mike, who had a

great impact on his children. He said, "It was an awesome story for them. When you do things for God, you have to put your trust in Him." He appreciated the motivation to try to get kids to think that way. He pointed out too that it was a challenging paradigm as a parent. "'We focus so much on their safety,'" Chris said. "But if we're serving the Lord, we trust God for all that."

Shortly after Mike's visit, Chris's oldest child spoke to a missionary in Guatemala and went down there to work. Certainly as a father, Chris was nervous. Mike served as an excellent example for the whole family.

This example only pushed the Lowes further in fulfilling the calling God had on their lives. They were already involved with Manna Global Ministries, an organization based in Clarksville, IN, with far-reaching ministries into Haiti, the Dominican Republic, and Africa. The Lowes had chosen to help in the Dominican Republic, having worked down there in various capacities six out of the last eight years. And they worked together as a family—sometimes all together and sometimes individually.

It started as basic mission work—fulfilling the physical needs of the people there and working in poor communities. They provided services as basic—but crucial—as pouring concrete floors. The Lowes took youth groups down there several times as well.

Eventually the ministry in the DR shifted its focus. In the economically poor city of Rio San Juan, MannaDR started a discipling school. In its second year, the outreach brought city kids in the 9th and 10th grade up to a small village where a missionary compound is located.

Chris said, "The trip is only five miles, but it takes nearly 45 minutes one way. That's the condition of the roads down there."

Students who attended the school received a full education. They studied math, science, and history. They even studied English; most of them already knew how to speak it, but the classes helped them improve. The school also weaved in a discipleship program, training the young men and women in living a Christian life. The school had three men and three women who served as mentors right there in the facility.

"Before, kids would come on Sunday or Monday night," Chris said. "It was a regular meeting, but only an hour here and an hour there. Now they are spending all day with young men and women."

The MannaDR project asked Chris and Angela to serve on an advisory board for the project. In this capacity they gave advice, kept an eye on the school, and mentored the team. Angela went down during the summer of 2012 and was amazed at the difference in the kids. The boys especially had become leaders—

leading the groups in devotionals, singing, and even a vacation Bible school."

The change was a welcome one to the individuals as well as the community. "A lot of them have rough home lives. This is our way of taking back the community," Chris said.

The chance for these children to go to college is uncommon. Public education is poor in this area and many of these students were already way behind, Chris said. "They had to do a lot of remedial work."

The reward of the program is that the community of people is strengthened. These students, with the chance to go to college, graduate and become part of a ministry to the greater community. This is even more so needed because there is no full-time missionary in the city at this point.

The Lowes live out their calling to missionary work, not just personally, but also as part of their church—as it has continued the efforts it began down there. The groups that went down in the summer of 2012 made a number of friends and had a great experience. Typically, when people come back from such a trip, they tend to forget it all. The Lowe's congregation, however, is helping to raise funds for the ministry down there. The youth group has already organized a 5k race and has several other projects in progress. Their immediate goal is to build a building for the school. Currently, the school has been using the dorms that missionary groups stay in during the summer. This gives them two classrooms in which to teach. The hopes are, with the funds the church raises, to build a building with four classrooms for them.

The mark of any journey is how it changes the one who takes it. The Lowes try to give of themselves to the world in time, effort, love, and most of all—faith. This can be seen in a seemingly random connection with a young man who arrived into their lives on a breaking-down, wrong-for-the-job bicycle and left on a brand new one, well-equipped for the journey ahead.

12 VIGNETTE: CLOVERDALE CHURCH OF CHRIST, SEARCY, AR

Long before Mike Baker ever heard of Cloverdale Church of Christ, the church was establishing its mission and paving a road that would be welcoming to him. "Compelled by Christ's love, we are devoted to family, expectant in mission, and renewed by God's Spirit," is the vision of the church. According to the church website, the mission of the church is "To glorify God by following in the footsteps of Jesus and being transformed into His image individually and corporately by reaching up to God, reaching out to others, and reaching in as we grow spiritually." If Mike Baker's visit was the only example of this, the church is clearly succeeding in its mission.

Brian Williams, the church's youth and family pastor, and John White, Brian's intern, were sitting together at McDonalds planning an event for the church. Normally, they wouldn't go to this particular McDonalds, but since they had to go to the nearby Wal-Mart, they chose to stop there. As they were finishing eating, Brian looked out and saw a scruffy looking guy in a green t-shirt riding a bicycle through town. He had a sign on his back, but was too far away for Brian to read it. Brian wasn't sure if the man was a biker, traveler, or a homeless man.

For a moment he lost the man in traffic, but then John noticed him crossing the street and coming into the McDonalds. John thought there was something different about this cyclist. It was not uncommon to see people on bicycles in Searcy, but he said that he could tell Mike had been on his bike quite a while. Then he saw the sign on Mike's back: "Bike For Christ."

"Now we're in business," John said.

They approached the man, introduced themselves, and offered to buy Mike Baker something to eat. As they sat down, they asked Mike to tell his story. The more he told them about his journey, the more they felt encouraged. It became clear to the two young men that this was not just a chance meeting.

"Being ministers, our first thought was 'How can we share this?'" John said.

Brian was scheduled to speak at a camp that day and asked if Mike wanted to join him. They took Mike to Bike City to get some work done on his bike. He went over to John's to shower and wash his clothes. Then they headed up to Camp Wildwood where Brian had been scheduled to speak and teach the Bible lesson to over 60 youth in attendance. He knew Mike had a great story and would be a living example of what the scriptures said. He didn't care about any plans he hadn't made. He just echoed a sentiment that so many people on Mike's journey had thought: "I didn't plan on Mike Baker."

"The kids were impressed," Brian said. "They fell in love with Mike. And just as much as he encouraged them, they wanted to encourage him. They took up a collection for him to help him on his trip."

"I knew he would do well," John said. "He has such an infectious personality. The kids just wanted to come up and talk to him. It was easy to sense that all eyes were on Mike."

John said that all of Mike's stories were about how God had provided for him. But he also had a sense that this was the first chance Mike had to give back what had been given to him.

Later on that day, Brian had to set up for his Wednesday night service. He would have to go back to the camp for the closing ceremonies, but he still wanted to give others a chance to hear Mike's story first hand.

"Let's keep this train going," John said.

John and Brian called and invited kids and their parents. They dragged Mike's bike up a flight of stairs to give his talk an added emphasis. There was a great deal of scrambling to make everything happen, but it ended up being a life-changing talk for many of the teens.

One teen wrote:

> *I met Mike around the time I started struggling with self harm and my relationship with God. I had just been diagnosed with Crohn's disease. I decided to go to church one Wednesday night and he was there and my youth minister had met him at McDonald's that day. He really inspired me. What he was doing amazed me. A few months after I met him I tried to commit suicide and was in the hospital. We sent Facebook messages back and forth and he let me know he was praying for me and gave me encouraging words and had other people praying for me. On New Year's he sent me a message right before me and my friend were going to try to overdose together. I feel like that was a sign from God. I'm so glad God put him into my life. He had his prayer group praying for me. I'm so blessed to have been able to meet him.*
>
> *—Abbey T., Searcy, AR*

It also changed Mike's life – in that audience sat Chris and Angela Lowe. John and Chris talked after the service and were both impressed at the faith Mike showed for someone as young as he was – young chronologically as well as spiritually. John had a sense that Chris and Angela wanted to provide a huge blessing for Mike. "I had no idea how huge," he said.

Even though these opportunities were some of the first large groups to which Michael had spoken, Brian remarked that his novice status didn't matter. "He had a good story. He had little time to prepare, so he just spoke from his heart. The kids saw that he was on fire for Christ."

Brian said that it was Mike's honesty and authenticity that stood out. He could tell that Mike did not like where his faith was before leaving on his journey. When he spoke, his audience knew that there was more to living for Christ than his old life showed. He wasn't content to sit back and play church.

"That," Brian said, "is something we can all recognize."

That second meeting connected Mike with Chris and Angela Lowe who purchased Mike a new bike when his old one began to show serious signs of wear. Though one could imagine such an event to be quite ceremonious, it was the exact opposite. Brian knew what was happening, but Chris and Angela didn't want to make a big deal out of it. They knew Mike was grateful. It was a special moment.

Later that night, John and his wife Jessi offered to give Mike a place to stay. John wasn't too concerned about letting a stranger stay in his house, but his wife was much more cautious. He had called Jessi earlier in the day to make sure everything was okay. She had no problems with it. Once again, this confirmed to John that this was a divine appointment.

Mike also had a long lasting effect on the teens. For some time after his visit, "the kids continued to reference Mike Baker. They talked about having faith like Mike Baker," Brian said. They continued watching Mike's journey as well, following him on YouTube and Facebook. There was a sense of "I know that guy and I know what he's doing." They were all certainly rejoicing with Mike when he reached San Francisco. "Here's a guy who set out to do something great and He did it!" Brian said.

The tangible results are not definite. Brian said, "With teens you plant seeds and at some point you see the growth." Brian said it's hard to see the impact because so much of it happens below the surface. Brian likened it to Mike's bike ride. "You see God putting different people in his life – seeing Him do that and knowing that God used everyone to do it."

Brian said he'll always remember Mike's talk as well. He'd been in those shoes – thinking there was more to the Christian walk than his present circumstances. Before coming to Arkansas, Brian had grown up in Michigan. He and his wife Tammy had two daughters, steady jobs, and worked for their church in various capacities. They had the idea of starting a youth ministry in their church, but the church wasn't ready to bring on someone.

They heard about Harding College - now Harding University - in Searcy, AR. The two-year program is actually a four-year degree condensed so that participants can get out of school and into the ministry. It's geared towards older students.

Tammy wasn't ready to go even through Brian was. The couple took a vacation down to Florida to pray and think about their decision. They decided to go for it: sell their house, quit their jobs, and leave the benefits behind. They weren't focusing on just themselves either: they had to worry about two kids, telling their immediate family and their extended family as well. They had to think about their two children and even their parents. Brian said one of the most challenging parts of the move was to tell the whole family ... especially having to tell his parents they were taking their grandchildren away.

After a great deal of prayer, Brian and Tammy quit their jobs, sold their home, raised support and left for two years of intense ministerial training.

The one part of the plan of which Brian was certain was that he didn't want to be a youth pastor and he didn't want to stay in the south. He felt like quite a "yankee" there. He didn't understand why people didn't drive right when the light turned green, why they looked at him strangely when he asked for a pop instead of a coke, and countless other subtle cultural differences.

That was 10 years before Mike.

It started with the uncomfortable feeling of sitting in church and doing nothing. Brian and Tammy had been involved in ministry and didn't feel right stopping. Some of his professors at Harding reassured him that he was "filling his toolbox" and biding his time. Brian still didn't feel comfortable. That's when a friend of his was leaving his internship position at Cloverdale Church of Christ. Brian hadn't considered youth ministry in some time, but the position was open … and it paid him a much-needed $300 per month.

Brian felt comfortable going into the interview. He knew that he wanted to "just do what God wants us to do; Go where God wants us to go." He had faith that God would provide for him. That faith has strengthened not just Brian, but his youth group as well.

Another way that Brian has a profound effect on those around him is by mentoring other youth leaders. John White came to him as part of Harding's internship program. He and Jessi had met at Harding, gotten married, and knew they would need to stop bouncing around and find a church. This happened at the same time Brian was looking for an intern. John stayed at Cloverdale for three years and has since gone on to work at West Side Church of Christ, a neighboring church still in Searcy, AR. This in itself was a divine blessing for John. Jessi had a job as a school teacher and didn't want to leave a great position in a town that she loved. John had known the realities that a position opening up in a town that had an influx of students looking for jobs was not a likely prospect. Yet, his jobs all seemed to line up at the right place and right time.

Brian and Tammy also felt the effects of living according to God's timing, but in terms of their family. They had their first two girls and Brian thought they were done. Tammy did not. The couple later had two more children—both boys. As if that wasn't enough, Brian and Tammy began to work with foster care agencies. The idea came from Chris and Angela Lowe, though it was embraced by the whole Cloverdale Church of Christ. They started with one baby and have added another one into their home. They had hoped to adopt the first child, but some of the details fell through. Though they were heartbroken, they understood the way the system works. The best they could do was to provide for a safe home environment.

Brian said they learned a valuable lesson: "Love these kids," he said. "You can't love them too much." In fact, Brian has the same advice for all parents – whether they are foster, adopting, or biological. "Be involved and stay involved all the way through." So many parents don't say it, but assume that spiritual training should be left up to the church. However, that doesn't mean parents have to sit on the sidelines. Brian suggests that parents volunteer, chaperone, and find other ways to know what's happening in their kids' lives.

13 COUNT IT ALL JOY

I left Searcy, Arkansas on Friday, July 29th, and had barely made it 10 miles when I checked my phone. I found some messages from Chris and Angela and just broke down in tears. My stop in Searcy left me feeling outright amazed at the generosity of people. The bike was beyond amazing—but the people there just kept giving. John sent me off with an iPod shuffle; I'm strongly contemplating not washing this one. He knew I liked Dave Matthews, so he put some music on it for me. I also left wearing a bright blue t-shirt with white writing on the front: "Crazy Love." The youth group I had just left donated it to me ... and it was covered in signatures from the teens there. Each one reminded me of how much they had touched my life. Emotions overwhelmed me probably 10 minutes, before I could start back down the road.

I spent the next 52 miles riding up and down hills—amazed at how easily the new bike handled. It rode smoother. The hills seemed less of a challenge. The handling responded so well. It was easily 10 times better than my old bike. Feeling good about everything, I called church after church hoping for a place to stay. Each one turned me down, so I ended up camping just off the road. It didn't bother me. "Who cares?" I thought to myself. I had been given such a blessing that it seemed nothing could bring me down.

When I stopped for lunch at the Leslie Café in Leslie, Arkansas, I noticed a splotch of grease on the frame of my bike. The bike chain rubbed it ever so slightly. I wrapped that part of the frame in some insulation I had found, determined I was going to make this bike last. I went into the café, ordered my food, and talked to Kimberly, my waitress, for probably a half hour. At the end, I walked out with another meal being paid for me. Blessings like this were so encouraging. In addition to the food, Kimberly also recommended a lake to me—a great place to swim and relax. I couldn't believe the way God's blessings just kept coming.

Shortly after that, things could have taken a downturn. Like so many of life's circumstances, it was just a question of what perspective I wanted to take. A metal wire punctured my tire and left it flat. I could have thrown a temper tantrum and let it get me down. Instead I counted another blessing: the tires on my new bike were infinitely easier to change. I could do the entire thing by hand in no time at all.

I continued towards the lake Kimberly had recommended, calling ahead for a camp site. It was $32 to camp—which was steep on my budget. I asked for a discount, believing it never hurts to ask. They could only go down to $25, but recommended the state park—its rates were cheaper. Thanks to their help, I ended up in Buffalo River State Park in Arkansas. The sites there only cost $12, but I only had a $20 bill. I walked through the campground looking for change and found a promising looking site. A van with "Baptist Church" stenciled on the side had parked there and about 15 people sat at tables around the site talking to one another. I figured one of them must have change, so I introduced myself and told them a little about my trip. Instead of breaking one of my $20's, they took up an offering and paid for my camp site. I couldn't thank them enough.

I set up my tent, sat down, and tried to decide what to do about food. The only place to eat was a 3-mile uphill ride. Even though I loved my new bike, after riding hills all day, I really didn't feel like doing it again. I just prayed and asked God if He would please feed me. Shortly after I finished that prayer, one of the campers next door came over and asked if I wanted their extra hamburger.

"Are you kidding me?" I laughed. I, of course, said "yes." I was amazed at how much better things were becoming for me.

While at the camp, a couple of 10-year olds came up to me and hounded me with questions. They asked about my water bottle, my bike, what I was doing, and so much more. They were extremely interested in my Camelbak and even wanted to try drinking from it. I smiled, remembered Jesus told his disciples they were to have faith like little children. These little guys weren't afraid of anything. They hadn't been introduced to great responsibilities and stress and stuff like that. They could do whatever they wanted. Best of all they had no limitations in their minds. I think that's why kids pick up games and other skills faster. They have no fears or doubts. We adults need to learn from them; we need to learn to live our lives that way. I remember wondering when we hit the point where we lose that childlike faith.

I'd like to say I slept peacefully, but nature seemed to have an alternate plan. In the middle of the night, I awoke to the sound of animals foraging and growling. I pulled out my survival knife just in case and peeked outside. Five or six raccoons were invading the campsites. They sniffed around my tent ... but I didn't have any food! I never considered my lack of food to be an advantage. My neighbors, on the other hand, were not so lucky. Despite putting their axe and their picnic table on top of the cooler, the raccoons still had a feast.

The next morning I awoke, freshened up, and headed towards Harrison. It was only 35 miles away, but I knew they would be difficult miles with a great deal of up and down hills. Twenty miles into my ride, I felt fatigue burning through my legs. At 25 miles, I came to a gas station and had to stop. I sat, panting for breath and massaging my legs, trying to convince them to try to make it the last 10 miles.

A man pulled up in a truck. "Probably pretty hot riding that bicycle?" he joked.

"Absolutely," I laughed.

"Where are you heading?" he asked me.

"I'm on my way to Joplin. You heading that way?"

"Nope, but I can take you as far as Harrison."

That was where I had planned to stay the night anyway! Praise the Lord! I jumped in the truck.

"Oh. Just please don't try to kill me," he said.

"Deal," I said, "as long as you promise to do the same."

"My name is Marvin."

"Mike."

As I rode along with Marvin, I talked to him about my story and my testimony. By the end of the ride, he invited me to stay with him ... I guess he wasn't worried about me trying to kill him anymore. Instead, I got a warm shower, a room to stay in, a place to do my laundry, and he even picked up dinner. In addition, he told me his son Justin would drive me forty-six miles to Branson the next day to get me out of the hills.

The next day, Justin had problems acquiring a truck, so Stacy, Marvin's wife, offered to let me stay another night. I stayed at their place while they went to work. She even gave me $20 to eat! The kindness of these new friends—amongst all the other ones—amazed me. I couldn't believe they trusted a complete stranger in their home.

I decided to use the time to rest both my body and my soul, so I watched a Francis Chan video. He was discussing I Cor 11:1, "Be imitators of me, just as I also am of Christ" (NASB). I thought about that and realized it would be amazing to be able to tell someone to "be like me." That took assurance. Paul had to be confident. I realized people have a difficult time understanding God—or even believing in Him—because they can't see Him. Once someone starts believing, it gets easier. With all the amazing blessings on my trip, I knew God was real and was with me. But others probably wouldn't be able to see that, or they would write it off as coincidence. That's where this verse comes in. Paul's confidence in telling people to follow him didn't come from himself, but from Christ. He wasn't being conceited; he was just sure of his relationship with Christ and wanted to bring others to a point where they could see that as well.

I felt the same way on this bike trip. I was confident I could make it, but my confidence didn't come from me. It came from the knowledge that God would carry me through to the end. I knew I would need that reassurance in the trip to come. It would be some of the hardest riding with some of the roughest terrain—from mountains to deserts and back again.

While resting at Marvin and Stacy's, I also continued reading my Bible, trying to beef up my faith while I could. The Bible is great for that. Paul says to one of his protégés, "All Scripture is God-breathed and is useful for teaching, rebuking, correcting and training in righteousness" (2 Tim 3:16). I read an interesting passage from another of Paul's letters. He says, "And You, who once were alienated and hostile in mind, doing evil deeds, he has now reconciled in his body of flesh by his death, in order to present You holy and blameless and above reproach before him" (Col 1:21–22 ESV). It talks about our communication with God. Before salvation—and unfortunately sometimes after it—our sin alienates us from God. It makes us run from Him, just like Adam and Eve did when they first sinned. They ran for the trees and tried to hide from God. The reverse is true too, though. When things are going well, our communication with God is constant. That was one of my favorite things about being on the bicycle. It was all about perpetual talk with God. I was excited to be God's vessel and show others how great He is. God does that by giving us what we need WHEN we need it. That can be a frustrating thing for a lot of people. We want to control things so much that we try to work God out of His job.

What really blew my mind about this concept is that the size of our need doesn't seem to matter to God. God provided a bike for me with no issue at all. As I was sitting at the house, I started to feel hungry and thought it might be nice to order a pizza. When Stacy came home, she had ... a pizza. Sometimes I think God does things like that just to have fun. I couldn't believe how great He was taking care of me.

Later, this stop would teach me a valuable lesson about appreciating God's daily blessings.

For now, it turned out that my day of being patient helped immensely. Marvin had Robert, a friend of his, drive me 90 miles to Rogers, MO, to get me completely through the Ozarks. That shaved at least three days off my riding.

So with all the incredible things that had happened on my trip, my faith should have been unshakable. I'd love to say that was the case. I'd love to say that nothing could get me down, but that wouldn't be the truth. And it certainly wouldn't be real. The only encouragement was that I was in good company. Even Christ's own disciples needed reminding from time to time.

So after getting a ride through the mountains, I started on my way ... and stopped less than two miles later—an abrupt stop ... a major abrupt stop. About 200 yards from an Arby's, a piece of tire debris jerked my bike to a skidding halt. Thankfully I was able to keep it upright. I inspected the damage and saw the remnants of something unidentifiable had caught in my rear derailleur and wrapped 180 degrees around my rear sprocket. Not only did it mangle my derailleur, but the force of the impact bent my frame. It took everything I could do to engage my faith again, laugh it off, and "Count it all joy."

I walked my bike to the Arby's so I could grab a bite to eat and find a bike shop. That walk garnered the attention of a man named Scott, who apparently knew that seeing a cyclist carrying a bike was not a good sign. He asked me what happened and told me he knew where the bike shop was. He even offered to take me there, and he already had a bike rack on his SUV! It was an amazing coincidence ... well, it was the first of many amazing "coincidences" which I later would know were the result of God putting the right people in the right place at the right time.

We arrived at the bike store and I found they were booked for two weeks on repairs. They had no clue when they would be able to repair my bike. Even when they could get to it, I knew I was in trouble. The derailleur on my old bike was a $15–20 repair. On this new one, it was over $200. Plus, they warned me that sometimes when they try to bend the frame back, it could snap.

Mike's bike, damaged from a tire wrapping around the derailleur

I stood there floored, completely paralyzed and not knowing what I was going to do. Was this it? Was this the end of my trip? Would I arrive home (and how would I even get there?) and tell people that I biked all the way to Rogers, Arkansas?

"Hold on a sec," Scott said. He left for a minute and returned with the manager, Nick. They happened to be good friends. Scott had told him my story and Nick said they would try to fix it right away. He understood the urgency of my situation. Unfortunately, he still wasn't sure if he could finish it that day. After a few hours of waiting for news, during which Scott went back to work, Nick told me I would have to wait until the next day.

God, as I learned on this trip, has a strange habit of going above and beyond anything I could ask. First, there just "happened" to be a man in the store who was a welder and overheard our conversation. He gave me his card and said to give him a call if the frame snapped; he'd take care of it. Second, since the repair was going to take until the next day, I called Scott. It turned out that my random good Samaritan, Scott, who just happened to stop and help a poor cyclist in trouble, also "just happened" to be the CEO of a major hospital in the area. His offer to stay wasn't just camping out on a lawn somewhere. He offered to put me up at the Embassy Suites hotel, but unfortunately it was booked—as was every hotel in the area. Instead I went to the hospital ... though just as a guest. I stayed in an unused wing with no patients. I had a bed and shower—and even got to eat the hospital food (which isn't as bad as people say). My pizza and chicken tenders dinner was actually quite tasty—and so was the ice cream I ate for dessert. The morning brought a breakfast of pancakes and eggs.

I still couldn't believe how God took what some people call a disaster and turned it into a whole series of miracles. When I picked up my bike from the shop—the bill had been covered. Scott and Nick made sure I returned to my trip and blessed me in amazing ways.

The Christian walk is a huge decision of attitude. People have a choice to make. A lot of them experience one bump in the road or one disaster and then they stray from God. I was trying to keep a positive attitude no matter what. Romans 8 says that all things—and that includes the ones we consider to be bad—work together for God's glory. I was reminded of the story of Joseph (Genesis 37–46). Over and over again, Joseph had obstacles to his dream. His own brothers planned to kill him, but then sold him into slavery instead. He rose to power, but then he was falsely accused of messing with his boss's wife and was thrown into jail. He helped a guy out and then the guy forgot about him. Finally, circumstances brought him to be the second most powerful guy in Egypt. It turned out all his trials prepared him for his big moment; he just had to keep heart until that moment arrived.

People have all kinds of desires they dream to do in life. Sometimes people's dreams are so much smaller than what God has prepared for them. For me, things like biking across the country and being a follower of Jesus Christ were not amongst mine when I was growing up. But I loved them! Other people have different dreams, but they are held back. There are all sorts of forces that do that: fear, lack of confidence, or a lack of vision. God can take care of all of those. He's an omnipotent God. That means no limitation can outrank God and His plan for our lives. No explanation can thwart Him. God can make all things happen!

14 PRAISING THROUGH THE TOUGH TIMES

On August 25th, my new derailleur and I left Rogers, Arkansas. It was an inexpensive one, just meant to get me back on the road. The one it had replaced needed some serious work. Nick at the bike shop said he would fix it and ship it home for me.

The next leg of the ride brought me into the full brunt of the summer heat. My goal was to reach a campground in Anderson, Missouri, rest there, and then continue on towards Joplin. I'd like to say how hot it was, but my iPhone actually put itself into standby because it was so hot. I didn't even know it would do that!

God continued to arrange chance meetings. About 10 miles into the ride, another Mike pulled over and offered me a bottle of water. He and I shared testimonies, and then he invited me to stay with him. It turned out he lived in Anderson, close to the campground for which I was aiming. He took me to his church and introduced me to Pastor Tom. I shared my testimony again with the pastor and then later with a Bible study of about 10 people. His topic for the night was "submission to Christ"—learning about giving our lives to Him. Shockingly, he actually used me as an example—quite a humbling experience. Pastor Tom prayed with me, gave me $10, and let me stay at the church. I was able to shower and do laundry while I was there as well.

While I stayed there, Mike and his friend Chris took me to Subway and bought dinner. We continued talking about what God had done for us. Mike had spent some time in jail, but while he was there, someone had introduced him to Christ and Christianity. After he got out, he built a giant cross, and was planning on carrying it across Kansas soon as a testimony of what Christ did for him. He and I had both heard the same response to the big journeys we were undertaking: "I admire what you're doing but I can't because ..." The "because" was always followed by some well-meaning reason. No matter what that reason was, it boiled down to the same thought process. It was an excuse.

Now, I'm not saying everyone has to bike across the country or carry a giant wooden cross—that's what we have chosen to do. Our call is not the same as other calls.

Other people have visions to start ministries, write books, or undertake some other humongous project. The key is that people have to be true to what God has called them to do. If they imitate other people's calls, they tend to fall flat on their faces, and either get tired of the journey or get turned away by the obstacles.

I heard someone say sometimes people get so busy doing the work of the Lord that they forget the Lord of the work. God didn't bless me because I was on a bike. I was certainly not the first and only person to bike across the country. People did that all the time. I even met several others along the route who were doing the exact same thing. God blessed me on that trip because I was using my call to seek Him. I was going about it my own way, in the way that He had made me. Anyone can do that! Anyone can seek God and put their faith and trust in Him. They just need to submit to God, do what He has called them to do, and not let excuses stand in the way.

The next morning, Mike sent me off with breakfast. I rode an amazing 37 miles without stopping, praising God for my new bike the entire way. I hit Joplin about 2:30 in the afternoon. I had researched the route of the tornado and decided to follow its path right down 20th street.

As soon as I hit town, my excitement plummeted, the shock of the scene pushing it far away from me. Words were completely inadequate to describe what had happened there. Even the pictures and videos I had seen on television paled in comparison to standing in the midst of it. I have never seen anything like it. Housing developments—not just houses, but entire neighborhoods—were completely gone. I passed an apartment complex where the tornado had ripped the entire second story off the building. Debris was piled everywhere—with no place to take it.

Just a small view of the destruction Mike saw in Joplin

The whole city had been destroyed. It was the craziest thing I had ever seen. Having been in the home improvement business, I had seen damage to homes. Typically I would have gone to Home Depot or another store to purchase materials and help fix it. In Joplin, the Home Depot itself was gone. Some workers had set up shop in a tent with some rudimentary supplies, but the store was nothing like it had been.

I took some time to talk to people. I met Joe, another cyclist, who was biking across Kansas trying to find some work. I also met Mike and Rose, a couple who had lost everything in the tornado; it took their house and vehicles. They even had to be rescued from the debris of their home. I shared a little of my story as well, and Mike gave me $20. It floored me! I didn't expect anything here. I wanted to figure out how I could help—not to take from them. But I knew God would bless this family. Maybe, like me, they had a reality check.

Mike (far left) and Joe (far right) with some of the Joplin citizens they met at a tent set up to provide supplies for those in need

My stay in Joplin made me want to make sure I lived my life in a way in which I knew I am satisfying God. I want to have no regrets when the end comes—which could be anytime. I often hear the expression, "we're not promised tomorrow," but it became quite evident standing in the midst of such destruction.

Not all of the destruction was from the tornado. I heard account after account of people who had taken advantage of the systems put in place to help this devastated town. People would collect insurance money and have volunteers rebuild and repair their homes. I heard of a preacher who stole washers and dryers - a ton of them - and sold them for profit. An emergency services responder had done the same with flat-screen televisions. Even churches, who should have been there to help, would often only stay for a week and then leave.

I camped in Joplin, and headed out in the morning. I wanted to stay in the worst way. I felt like I could lend some of my talents here, but as I looked around I couldn't even decide where to start. I knew the helplessness I felt was only a fraction of what others were feeling. I realized if I started helping, I might not ever leave. This was not my calling, it was someone else's— and that was a hard thought to admit.

The next day I put Joplin behind me physically, though it would also stay in my mind—probably forever. I forced myself to pedal away. Though the flat ground did not offer much of a challenge, the head wind continually pressed against me. At the end of the ride, I pitched my tent at a cheap campground. While there, I shared my story with the lady who worked in the office, and she paid for my site. I rode into town to grab dinner at Pizza Hut and stopped by the Wal-Mart to pick up some supplies. I ran into Joe, the cyclist I had met back in Joplin, and I bought him lunch—a nice change—and invited him back to my camp site. Joe didn't even have a tent; he was really roughing it. We cooked hot dogs for dinner and passed the time together with some enjoyable conversation. Being around another person lifted my spirit. I thought about it and realized God puts people together for a reason. We need to surround ourselves with people who are filled with the Holy Spirit and are what we want to be. If we're around negative personalities and people who do bad things, they will bring us down.

Even though Joe and I parted ways, I needed that boost the next day. It was 105 degrees in the daytime (which was only 10 degrees warmer than it had been the night before). I had everything I needed: water, food, prayer, and Jesus. Still, it was a hard day's ride. I fought headwinds—which were perfectly normal for Kansas. All the winds go west to east and I would be riding into them the whole way. It was an odd experience to not be able to coast downhill. The headwinds actually cancelled the downhill effect. I also found more gravel paths—not the ideal riding surface. I found smoothness in the tire tracks from cars that had gone before me. When I couldn't ride in those, I once again praised God for my new bike. On my old one, the rough ride would have been bone-jarring and potentially dangerous. While it wasn't comfortable now, it was certainly much easier than before.

To make matters more difficult, the towns here were much farther apart than they had been out east. And it wasn't uncommon to find towns so small they didn't have restaurants. In Cambridge, Kansas, a town of 82 people, I called all the churches in the community—both of them! One did not answer. The other one had a van driving to pick up people in the next town. They included me in their pick up schedule and stopped at a gas station. Knowing stops were few and far between, I picked up two gallons of water, two Gatorades, four granola bars, and a bag of Chex mix. The church's van driver offered to pay for it all. It was incredible. Later, I went to their church service and told my testimony. They gave me $100 and said I could stay at the church. A couple there offered their shower and laundry as well.

The next day brought more of the same difficult riding conditions, though it was even harder than the previous day. The first 5 or 10 miles everything was okay; the wind was strong, but at least it was a crosswind. Once I turned north, the story changed. I rode headlong into 20 mph straight-line winds. I set my sights 27 miles ahead to a cafe in Leon, Kansas. The first 9 miles seemed to take forever. I probably averaged 5 mph and could barely stay on the road. I had to stop four times. The fifth time, I rested for 20 minutes and considered calling it quits. This time there were no trucks from which I could hitch a ride.

Just as I decided to give it one more try, a song came on my iPod, the chorus of which says, "Oh, how He loves us," talking about God's immense love for His children. I had a revelation during this time. We should always praise God for being God, not just when He blesses us. God always deserves our worship and his glory. He wants us to praise Him even in the tough times. I've had so many blessings, how could I get down or give up on one tough day? God wants us to love him even when the times are tough. Life has its rough patches, but we always know that no matter what is going on in our lives, God is still the Almighty and always will be. He always deserves His Glory.

So I decided those winds weren't going to stop me. I felt a burst of energy and fought against them for the next 18 miles. Just as I reached the end, the winds died down. Exhausted, I rolled into the Leon cafe and knew I was in a good place: they had written John 3:16 on their window.

The Leon Cafe in Leon, KS, displaying the scripture verse John 3:16 *For God so loved the world that he gave his only begotten Son, that whosoever believeth in him shall not perish, but have everlasting life.*

I smiled knowing God's love had pushed me through the difficult times. It turned out the cafe also doubled as a Full Gospel church. I told them my story and they blessed me with lunch.

My faith and my stomach full, I rode another sixteen miles, aiming for an Assembly of God campground. I arrived there to find two men working on a truck. I told them my story. Pastor Bobby was going to put me up in the church office. Instead, they let me stay in the camping facilities—complete with bunk beds, a shower, and a bathroom—all for free.

I had planned to stop in Wichita the next day, looking forward to three major comforts. First, I wanted to stop at Best Buy to pick up an external hard drive so I could take the media files off my phone. Not only was my phone starting to run out of space, but I also didn't want to run the risk of losing them again—like I had when my phone fell off my bike. Second, I needed to visit a bike shop to pick up some supplies and parts. Third, I really wanted Chipotle ... and I had a sneaky suspicion God wanted to give it to me for free.

.

15: FALLING AND SOARING

I had a feeling God wanted to give me some free Chipotle; I had a huge craving for it. On Tuesday, August 9th, I started out my morning at McDonald's for breakfast. I signed onto my Facebook account and had a new friend request from a guy I used to work with. He also sent me a message and said he wanted to pay for some Chipotle for me! He ordered it online; all I had to do was bike there and pick it up. Praise God.

My stop at Best Buy wasn't as successful. We spent 2 hours trying to transfer my videos, but we couldn't get them onto the hard drive I had bought from them. Frustrated, I decided to abandon the effort for the time being and head towards the bike shop ... as soon as I figured out where it was. I asked a stranger for directions and he was able to point me in the right direction—and he even gave me five dollars!

More than that, it started me on one of the most incredible parts of my journey. I had no clue what was in store for me when I entered the Bicycle Pedaler in Wichita, KS. It seemed mundane at first. They gave my bike a checkup and I picked up some spare tubes. I talked to the owner, Ruth Holliday. She and her husband, Bob, had gotten married and rode to California together for their honeymoon. She told me the last person who had the same tires as mine rode on them for 4500 miles with no flats. I already was doing infinitely better in that department since I had been given my new bike. That was great news.

I called ahead to the next stop to find a campsite, but they were $20 each. I tried the church route once again, but no one was available. I finally found a state park I could stay at for $8. It was 33 miles away, so the ride should have been easily do-able. So I took off down the road.

I know I said my stop in Wichita was an incredible adventure. And if my day had gone the way I had planned it, I would have passed through and never known better. Instead, I had made it about 8 miles down the road when my plans abruptly—and somewhat painfully—changed.

About 6pm, I was cruising down the sidewalk, moving at a decent clip of 15–17 mph, and I saw a puddle. It must have been the little boy in me—the little guy who always loved splashing in mud puddles—that gave me the idea. I had my mud guards on the new bike, so I figured I'd have some fun and fly through the puddle.

Apparently that puddle had been there for some time. The sidewalk beneath it had grown mossy, which acted like an ice patch to my tires. As soon as I passed over it, my bike flew out from under me. I slammed down with all my weight, sliding across the concrete on my right side for about 15 feet. The force of the fall shocked me—probably more than it hurt me. It had been so long since I had fallen off a bike—especially doing something so simple. One man stopped and asked me if I was okay. I thought I was, so I waved him onward.

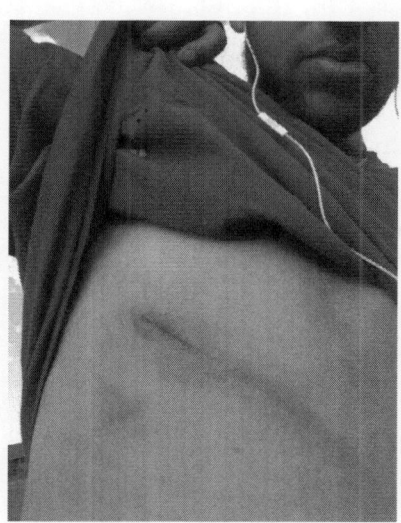

I took a quick inventory, hoping I hadn't broken anything or was seriously injured in some other way. The fall left an eight-inch scrape across my chest, drawing a little blood—ruining my shirt in the process. My bike didn't fare as well. The fall broke my rear brake

Mike shows off the scrape from his wreck

lever and gear shifter. This would not be an easy or cheap repair and it was serious enough that I had to fix it before I could go further. I forced myself to look at the bright side: it could have been much worse. I had no bent rims or spokes and my frame looked okay. My saddlebag was scuffed pretty badly, but it had also protected my new derailleur.

By the time I inventoried everything, it was getting close to 6:30pm. I tried the next bike shop on my route, but it was already closed. Something in me told me to call Ruth from Bicycle Pedaler back in Wichita, but I really didn't want to retrace the miles I had just ridden. Plus the shop was already closed. I punched the number into my phone and was shocked when Ruth answered. Even though she had already closed up shop, when she saw a Columbus, Ohio number pop up, she thought it might be me and answered the call. I explained the situation, not knowing how she could help.

As usual, my imagination could not fathom what God was about to do through Ruth. She came and picked up me and my bike. Since it was already so late, she let me stay with her and her husband. She also bought me dinner at Wendy's. Ruth had a replacement part for my bike, though it wasn't as good as the part had been originally (now it was about 100 times better than the broken part, since it actually worked). It took her most of the next day to fix it, which wasn't a terrible thing for me since it had rained most of the morning. Still, she offered to let me stay another night. In addition to that piece of her amazing generosity, she also did the repair at cost for the part and did not charge me labor. Once again, God's blessings seemed incredible.

And yet, God was about to do even more than that.

Bob, Ruth's husband, was a pilot with a glider plane— which was exactly what it sounded like: a craft that looked like a small airplane, but had no motor of its own. Instead, a plane with an engine tows it up into the air. When they both reach a good altitude, the glider releases the tow strap and enjoys a long float down to earth again. An experienced pilot can stay in the air all day long without a drop of fuel.

Bob needed help loading his plane up at the airport—which was located at a small private airport about 45 miles west of where we were. I was glad just to be able to help repay his kindness; after all, he and Ruth had been amazingly helpful to me. In addition, though, helping Bob would get me a good head start on the next leg of my journey. I had planned on camping at the airport and getting an early start the next day.

God still managed to do more.

I helped Bob with his plane and then started to pitch my tent. While we were there, another plane took off and flew away.

"Man, I would love to be able to fly someday," I

said.

"Well," Bob said, "I wish I would have known that, because I have a few planes back in Wichita I could have taken you up in."

I felt a slight feeling of disappointment. I would have loved to make that happen.

Then Bob said, "You know, nothing's set in stone around here. Pack up your tent."

God's blessings overflowed during that part of the trip. Bob took me up in a small plane. We did touch and go landings at four different airports around the area. Then he gave me the controls! In one day I went from riding a bike to actually flying a plane. For a half-hour, I was completely free, flying through the sky. He even let me hold the controls as he helped me land the plane. It didn't get better than that ... or so I thought.

Bob's plane is ready to take Mike on one of the most amazing rides he'd ever experienced

Bob and Ruth let me stay another night with them and I planned on heading out the next morning. Instead, the next day Bob let me experience something I may never get to do again. He took me up in his glider plane.

It turned out Bob was one of the best pilots and could stay up in a glider for 6 or 7 hours at a time. This one was a little different than the prop plane. We started by putting on parachutes—that put things into perspective for me. Another plane towed us for the first 15 to 20 minutes. Then we pulled the cable to detach. My stomach dropped for a moment as I realized we had no power—only the wind and an experienced pilot. It was a mixture of freedom and dread at the same time.

Mike is all buckled in, has his parachute on, and is ready to head to the sky in Bob's glider plane

Mike's view from Bob's glider as it is being towed into the air

Then Bob started with the acrobatics. He did three separate loops, as well as other flying maneuvers. One of the craziest ones was flying straight up then turning and dropping sideways back towards earth. He offered to let me take the controls again, but after the last stunt, I told him I would pass. My stomach was reeling just a little bit more than I was comfortable with. I had grown accustomed to being on the road, not in the air.

Fortunately, it had recovered by the time I got back to Bob and Ruth's house since they had ribs and corn on the cob waiting. They even fed me a pancake breakfast the next morning.

Just in case all that wasn't enough, they gave me a

mirror and rear reflector to help with my safety when I was riding. The mirror clipped onto my sunglasses and would give me a great perspective on what was behind me. On a whim, I asked Bob if the shop carried trailers. Bob showed me his old trailer in his garage and sold it to me for $225, though it was easily worth $350.

It was worth every penny. Having most of my gear off the bike just made the ride easier.

Once again, this leg taught me a huge spiritual truth. When I crashed on my bike, I had to make a conscious decision with my attitude. I had to acknowledge that sometimes bad stuff happens. If someone had asked me if I wanted to crash, I would have laughed at them. Of course I didn't want to crash. It embarrassed me. It hurt. It frustrated me. But it also opened the door to a series of blessings that I could never—in a million years—have predicted.

Proverbs is a book in the Bible with tons of wise sayings. I love one in particular: "Trust in the LORD with all your heart and lean not on your own understanding; in all your ways submit to him, and he will make your paths straight" (Pro 3:5–6 NIV). I trusted God, even in the middle of my accident. God took something like that and made it work for good—taking me to all new heights ... literally.

Mike's new setup for his trip: bike, trailer, and backpack with sign

16: CHANCE ENCOUNTERS

The next leg of my route was a crisscross of "chance" meetings. God intersected my path with the most interesting cast of characters. I left Wichita a little late and thought I'd take a leisurely ride. It was Saturday, August 13th, and the August heat bore down on me. It didn't take long to run into my first encounter: an Irishman named Brian. He was a cyclist too, but he had flown into Oregon and was riding the opposite way. He was a singer as well and had a gig in Hutchinson, Kansas—a town I had passed about 13 miles previously. I decided having a companion was worth the 13 miles of backwards riding, so he and I joined together and rode back the way I had come. Brian needed to get his bike repaired too, so we found a bike shop together and stopped there. While we were at the shop, we told the people there about our journeys. They knew we would need a place to stay and had keys to a nearby church that would open its doors for travelers.

This "church" wasn't what I had been used to seeing on my trip. While it certainly looked normal upstairs, it had a facility in the basement set up specifically for traveling bicyclists. It turned out we were on the Trans-America bicycle route and it would be common to see these types of setups. Everything in this bike hostel was perfect. They had a shower with fresh towels, and even had two beds set up with freshly-washed sheets and blankets. They had televisions for us to watch—it had been quite some time since I had sat and watched TV. They even had a stocked refrigerator with drinks in it. And the church had signs on everything telling the bikers to take and use what they needed. There were giant posters on the walls signed by all the fellow bikers who had passed through, telling about their journeys. It was an awesome place to be.

The church had everything we needed, and, thanks to Brian, it also had some amazing Irish music. He had a great melodious voice. It was a strange feeling having a piece of Ireland right in the middle of Kansas.

Despite the serene scene, my spirit still felt restless. I couldn't put my finger on it, but I just felt like something was wrong. When I got back to the church, I called Conrad and Tom and had them pray. About an hour later, my phone rang. It was Stacy - Marvin's wife from my stay back in Harrison, AR. Marvin, who had joked around about me not killing him, had died in his sleep that day. Stacy called me, not just to let me know, but to thank me for being part of the last week of his life - even though we had no idea at the time. I thanked her for her call and told her I was sorry for her loss - not sure of what else to say.

The next day, my mind still back with Marvin, I went to the church service in Ellenwood, KS, and had a chance to talk about my trip afterwards. Various people there gave me $45. Another night, I stayed in a Roman Catholic Church. After that, I hit another dry spell with my lodging. All the churches I called did not answer or declined. One church said they did not have "adequate facilities" to host me. I had to laugh—all I really needed was a patch of grass. I just stayed in a rest area that night.

The terrain across Kansas continued to challenge me. The sun blazed for days that seemed endless. The wind continually peppered my face with debris. At one point, I caught a glimpse of my face. It shocked me to see the pale lines my sunglasses covered amid the scorched redness of my face. I found few gas stations or restaurants, so I had to adjust my way of thinking and remember to stock up on supplies at each one. At one of those gas stations, I asked the attendant if they had many riders. He mentioned another bicycling couple had just passed through about 10 minutes before me. They were heading west as well. I thought it might be interesting to ride with them if our paths crossed, so I just prayed God would orchestrate the meeting.

My trials continued as I called several churches and had each one turn me down. Finally, I had a breakthrough with the third church I called. I asked if I could just stay on a patch of grass. They said, "We're going to do better than that!"

I only had to make it another 25 miles to Tribune, Kansas, so I set my sights on the church and continued down the road. During that burst, when I stopped for a drink, I had a chance to meet the biking couple. Their names were Katie and Cheney. They had just gotten married, were 28 and 29 years old, and were traveling a year long journey together. They had travelled as far as Thailand, had hiked Mt. Kilimanjaro, and now they were going to bike from Mississippi to Los Angeles. Since we were going the same direction, but finishing in different places, our paths would be similar. We all thought it would be fun to ride together as much as possible.

At one stop we hung out together, opting to stay at a park. The townspeople there said we could get a key to a bath house from the town courthouse. We showered and ate, then went and shot pool to pass the time and relax a little. It was fun, but I woke up at 4:30 in the morning sick to my stomach. It passed in the morning, but it made me aware of yet another blessing I had taken for granted during this trip: my health. I had been—for the most part—in fairly good health. I knew things could change quickly, but I just didn't want to let myself think about that. I continued trusting in God to make sure I had all I needed.

The next morning Katie, Cheney, and I biked towards Colorado. My spirit lifted with every mile. Kansas had been such a difficult trek, and crossing the Colorado border was one of the best feelings of this leg. It only made a little difference geographically, but it was a huge benefit to my mental state. We stayed at a church in Ordway, Colorado—enjoying the coolness of the air conditioning. We continued to press onward until Saturday, August 20th. After lunch at Chipotle, we parted ways. There was a slight chance we would meet up again. Regardless of whether or not we did, Katie and Cheney were welcome friends on the trip.

Alone again, I called churches to find a place to stay, but no one answered. I paid $13 to stay at a campground, leaving me with just $14. I did have the epiphany while riding, however, that I have had a lot of people praying for me daily. I decided I wanted to start a prayer time in which I could pray for what other people need. After all, there was strength in numbers.

As I drew close to Canyon City, Colorado, I looked for a place to stay and found more comfort with strangers. I came across a Vineyard Church camp where

Bill, the operations manager, allowed me to stay.

While there, I realized I was so close to the Royal Gorge—home of one of the world's highest suspension bridges. Almost every fiber of my being wanted to check it out ... every fiber, except my legs. Even though I was only two miles away, that had to be doubled. Four miles on a bike meant a lot of time and energy. I knew as I entered into the foothills and headed towards the mountains of Colorado, every mile would count. Missing out on the opportunity to see the gorge was one of my few regrets for the trip, but I knew it was necessary to reach my goal.

I learned a valuable lesson with this. The Bible says, "Therefore, since we have so great a cloud of witnesses surrounding us, let us also lay aside every encumbrance and the sin which so easily entangles us, and let us run with endurance the race that is set before us, fixing our eyes on Jesus, the author and perfecter of faith, who for the joy set before Him endured the cross, despising the shame, and has sat down at the right hand of the throne of God" (Hebrews 12:1–3 NASB). That "encumbrance" was what I was experiencing. Our lives have so many "good" opportunities come up, but God has never been about the good—He gives the "best." Besides, who was I to complain that I missed one small opportunity when I had been given so many amazing ones I never expected?

As I was packing up the next morning, I had the

chance to meet Bob—who was standing up on a balcony at the time. I told him my story and he called about 10 adults together. They all prayed for me. I had begun to worry again, knowing I only had $14 in my pocket at that point. I shouldn't have worried. Even though Bob had no clue how much money I had, God did. Bob came up to me and said he just "felt it in his spirit" to give me something. He handed me 100 dollars. It should not have surprised me; God had been so good to me on the trip—but it still never ceased to amaze me.

Of course, not all of my meetings were "chance" meetings with strangers. God always kept me in touch with familiar people. When I ran out of money again, I talked to a friend back home. She gave my mom money to put in my account. The money situation frustrated me, but then I realized it's better to be broke and depend on God than to be rich and not know God at all.

I also had a place to stay in Salida, Colorado where my best friend Conrad's sister, Magda opened her home to me. To get there I had to ride long uphill stretches against the wind. It was a tough 60 miles, but it was so worth it when I arrived at Magda's house. I had a chance to shower. I took a moment and looked in the mirror. I knew my hair had been getting longer—I could feel the heat it held while I was biking. My beard was starting to fill out as well. And it all was difficult to keep clean when I didn't have access to regular showers. I took the opportunity to shave both; I was eager to get rid of them.

The stay at Magda's was a great refresher. I had the chance to get a pizza ... which I had been craving for quite some time. I also used her computer to catch up with friends and family—much easier to use than my small iPhone screen.

And like so many other stops before, this one would be more than basic room and board. Magda worked for a zip line tour company. They had six lines, the longest of which was 700 feet long and 300 feet above the canyon. It would have been something to hang suspended from a high tension wire in a harness and almost fly over Colorado. A tour cost around $90 and there would have been no way I could have afforded it.

But my connection with Magda gave me the chance to experience it for free—praise God! Once again, the change in perspective amazed me. I had been accustomed to seeing Colorado at ground level. The next thing I knew, my feet dangled far above the ground as I coasted using only gravity, looking down at the breathtaking sights below.

And, if that wasn't enough, the second day I stayed with Magda, there was a huge bike race in town that drew many of the best riders around—including Lance Armstrong. I had the chance to see the 129 racers off for the first of five stages—98 miles over the mountains. Racing bikes—that was something so different than the riding I had been doing. I was working towards endurance for a trip that had taken three months so far.

As I arrived back at Magda's, I checked in with Katie and Cheney again. They were in town as well, and Magda offered to let them stay too. We connected and took care of our bike check-ups. Later that evening, we watched the movie, *Bicycle Dreams*—a true story about the Race across America (RAAM)—a 10 day, 3000 mile race from the Pacific coast to the Atlantic. Only about half the people who attempted the race even completed it, and some people had actually died on the race. Athletes considered it to be one of the toughest sporting events in the world. More people climbed Mt. Everest than finished the RAAM. One man who did it only slept a total of 11 hours through the whole trip.

The next day we bid farewell to Magda and continued our journey. I quickly learned how thankful I was that God had sent Katie and Cheney. We stood at the base of Monarch Pass: 18 miles uphill to 11,312 feet above sea level. Any physics teacher can tell his or her students slope is rise over run. It's something entirely different when biking both rise and run. I had biked up hills. I had even biked up steep hills. Monarch Pass would be the hardest hill of my journey so far.

Thankfully I was not alone. Katie, Cheney, and I talked about *Bicycle Dreams* and the elation we felt while watching it. We remembered how the dedicated riders had been so amazing to watch. So we stopped, looked each other in the eyes, and made a pact. We were going to ride up Monarch pass without a foot touching the ground. No matter who fell behind, no matter how long it took, and no matter what obstacles we encountered, we were each going to try to reach the top in one shot.

Making the pact was easy; keeping it would be hard.

I fought four different stages on my way up the hill. Every one of them was a mental battery where my mind and my body wrestled over who had control. In the first section, pain split through my knees so strongly that they both felt like they would buckle. They strained under the combined force of my body and gravity as I ordered them each—one at a time—to keep pushing. I never left low gear. When I hit the point that I felt I couldn't go any further, I looked down and realized I had only made it a third of the way.

That started the second stage of the climb. Every pullover spot enticed me to stop. I felt the weight of my trailer pulling me back. I wanted nothing more than to run off the road, collapse, and let my body rest—the way I had seen Frank do it on the way to Florida. Cheney had already fallen behind; I could just quit too. But Katie was right behind me. She kept pushing me, not letting me stop.

As the screams of pain from my body started to drown out Katie's cheers, I was ready to give in and stop.

Just then, I saw the sign indicating we were only six miles from the summit. I knew I couldn't quit. The third stage began at that point: knowing I was so close, but still had so much to go. These were the hardest six miles of the journey, but Katie and I would not allow ourselves to stop. We continued to push each other to ride through the pain, counting off each mile marker as we passed it.

The fourth "stage" only lasted one mile ... the steepest of them all. I felt the altitude—the thinning air that never seemed to quite have enough oxygen. I looked around and saw how sparse the trees had become. Soon, the road ahead of me disappeared over the horizon, rather than stretching endlessly upwards.

And, before I knew it, Katie and I reached the top of Monarch pass. Four hours had passed in the agony of the struggle in which every minute had mattered. We calculated it and realized our pace was four and a half miles an hour—not much faster than a brisk walking pace. And yet,

Mike takes a moment to ham it up in celebration of his climb to the summit of Monarch Pass

we felt incredible—having overcome a huge obstacle in our trip.

The best part of the uphill battle ... is the downhill coast. After we had all rested (and Cheney had caught up) we pointed our bikes downwards and enjoyed 20 minutes of some of the easiest riding we had done as we coasted downhill. In fact, the next 40 miles were by far some of the easiest riding I had experienced at this point of the trip. With a temperate breeze and gentle slopes, we headed towards a place to stay for the evening.

The next day brought more chance encounters. A storm hit and stranded us at a gas station. After 20 minutes of trying to hitch a ride, we decided to brave the rain and attempt a long downhill stretch with a small shoulder. Fortunately, just as we started, a truck saw us, stopped, and the driver - Galynn - offered to give us a ride. The downhill stretch would have ended quickly, yielding to two big climbs. Galynn's help was quite welcome help in light of the hill we had just ridden.

Looking back, a couple of things amazed me. First, I was in awe at the "chance encounters" God put in my path. I would never have made it up that hill without Katie's encouragement. I found friendships and kindred spirits that still warm my heart and soul to this day when I think of them. Secondly, I was amazed to think of how much time factored into these encounters. Five minutes of time or stopping at one restaurant over another could have completely changed the sequence of my trip.

The reverse is true too, unfortunately. I never knew when those times would stop. I heard a news report from home while I was on my trip. Not far from where I live, a man shot and killed his girlfriend. Afterwards, when the police were trying to arrest him, he resisted and they had to shoot and kill him. I thought he probably wasn't expecting to die that day. Yet these things happened all the time all over the world.

The bottom line was, as I thought about it, we never know what's going to happen in any given day. From an earthly standpoint, things could go well or poorly. From God's point, everything works for good. That's the difference Jesus Christ can make in people's lives. That's why I want everyone to know Jesus. Granted, it helps us to be ready for the afterlife; Christ made it abundantly clear we have an eternal life and this temporary one is preparation for it. But it also helps us in this life. People always are nervous about how to make their ends meet and how to make sure they have all they need. I started out this trip with $300 and by this time, I had been given over $1500 by strangers and had been blessed with a $1300 bicycle. God is interested in providing for us even in this temporal existence.

17: HOMES AND HOSPITALITY

By the 26th of August, Katie, Cheney, and I had picked up another rider. Like me, Alex was biking across the country, but he was going the opposite direction— actually starting in San Francisco. As another example of how unprepared I was for the trip–and how God still provided for me—Alex introduced me to Adventure Cyclist maps. The Adventure Cycling Association (ACA) (http://www.adventurecycling.org) produces these maps. ACA is a non-profit organization of over 45,000 members, headquartered in Missoula, MT and is helping with the development of an official US Bicycle Route System. It is doing this by making maps designed just for cyclists. More than just showing where to go, they have notes about elevations—which are crucial for riders. They also show facts about historic towns, scenic stops, and locations of national parks. Certain town maps list places to stay as well as show grocery stores and gas stations. And, as I was discovering, some towns were so small, they didn't even have a place to stop for water. These maps showed the best places to stock up on critical supplies to avoid being caught without them. Since Alex was finished with his maps from the first part of the journey, he gave them to me to help me get to San Francisco. Looking at the small handful of maps, it hit me how close I really was at this point.

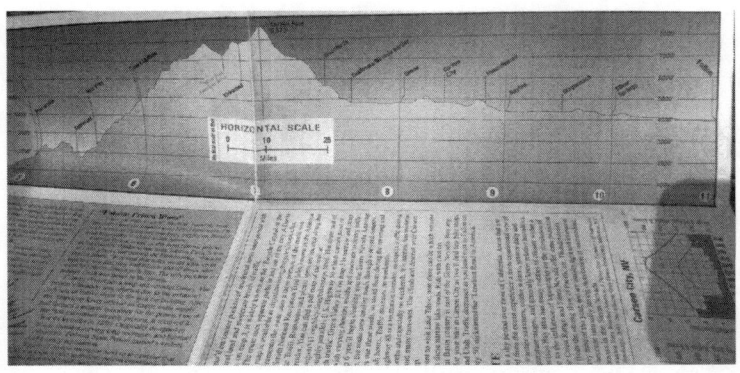

Mike's ACA map showing the last leg of his trip

In Montrose, Colorado, we met a Warm Showers host, Jenny, as she opened her home to Katie, Cheney, Alex, and myself, giving us all a place to stay and shower, and even gave us a handful of Cliff bars—a great staple for the road.

"Warm Showers" was another touring cyclist help I hadn't known about when I started, but had helped me immensely. It's a website-driven hospitality network—www.warmshowers.org. There are basically two types of people on Warm Showers—cyclists and hosts (and a lot of people are both). A host indicates where they are and what availability they have to host people. A cyclist can get on the website, contact that host, and see about staying with them. Most hosts allow camping on the lawn, but a lot of them open their homes as well. In addition, they also offer food and services such as showers and laundry.

Warm Showers is an amazing network started by Terry Zmrhal and Geoff Cashman in 1993. They had a great idea, but the technology to back it up hadn't been invented yet. In 1996, Roger Gravel found the original list and began updating it. By 2005, Randy Fay had given it the technological boost it needed using the database-and-map web model. Randy and "a small but dedicated" group of volunteers manage the site now. By the time of my trip, they had over 14,000 hosts and 25,000 members.

And then it hit me. This was the same thing I was doing, but in reverse. Instead of going out and meeting all sorts of new people, these people were opening their homes to others. It took just as much faith to do that—and probably more. Like me, who wasn't getting paid or even sponsored in any way, Warm Showers hosts don't charge for their services. That takes faith as well. And like me, who was riding about sharing my story for others to hear, each of the Warm Showers hosts has his or her own story. Gathering together with other people is an excellent way to share those stories.

Hospitality is so important to humanity. It's a way of lending a hand to others no matter how similar or different they might be. I thought about all the different people who had taken me in during my trip and how giving they had been. It seemed like such a simple concept, but there were certainly those who did not subscribe to that same line of thinking. As I pictured many of the people I had contact with back home, I think I could have counted on one hand how many would open their homes to strangers - and I wasn't sure if I would have been one of them. I hadn't even known there were people biking through Ohio who might need a place to stay for a night. I couldn't do a great deal for them, but I knew I wanted to be a place of refuge—offering a warm bed, a hot shower, and a filling meal to someone in need. I thought it would be so great to have the time and resources to offer care and help. I knew I wanted to do so much more—for other people and for God!

After staying with Jenny, we woke up the next morning and all parted ways. It seemed so surreal. Katie and Cheney had been with me through some of the roughest parts of the trip. Alex, even though we had just met, was still great to have around and his experience helped my own journey. And yet, with one last breakfast, they were all gone.

Once again, I had to focus on my trip. I wasn't here to make friends—even though I had made some awesome ones. I was here to complete a journey. If I let myself focus on the people I met, I would never reach my goal. So, I was determined to find new contacts. Using the Warm Showers site, I found Ed in Grand Junction and called ahead to him. After a relatively easy 63 mile stretch, I arrived at his place. He wasn't home, but he told me where his spare key was and let me go in and get a shower, do my laundry, and relax. Later, he and his wife Maggie brought pizza for dinner. Again, the way God put the right people in my path continued to amaze me. Here a complete stranger let me into his house and even provided for me, asking nothing in return. I couldn't ask for more than what God had used Ed to give me.

And yet, God provided.

Ed offered to let me stay a second night while we took a short day trip, biking around the Colorado National Monument all the way up to about 6000 ft. A couple times every year the local government closed the roads to allow cyclists and hikers to enjoy the sights. I just "happened" to be there at one of those times! This reminded me again that I was on God's time schedule. If I tried to calculate the perfect day to arrive at the Colorado National Monument from Ohio, via two other stops, while traveling with the unpredictability of bicycle travel ... nah, there's no way I could have planned this part of the trip. Yet God put me in the right place at the right time. I suddenly had great company from a myriad of other cyclists. One of the best parts of being able to cycle the monument was that I got to do it with no gear on my bike—something I hadn't enjoyed since the run to Florida. I had started the trip with everything on my back, then I switched my load to my saddlebags, and later I put it on my trailer. Now, as I pushed my bike past 40 mph, I could do so completely unencumbered! I hadn't realized how much my gear weighed me down until I was able to cycle without it.

The monument was indescribable: beautiful carvings of rock stretching towards the sky. I had been so used to Ohio terrain, that I didn't realize how far the horizon could actually stretch. We would stop and look out and watch the terrain roll outward for miles upon miles. At one point I looked out west and slightly south—the direction I was heading—and realized I still had a long road ahead of me. There would be nearly 100 miles between the monument and Moab, Utah. That 100 miles held some extremely difficult terrain—long deserts and few stops. But I knew God would still be with me.

The next day, Ed and Maggie rode the first 10 miles with me—taking me out towards Highway 50. It would be the only easy part of the ride. I pushed through wind for the next 30 miles—serious headwinds, so strong I had to pedal downhill just to stay moving. On top of that, even despite the wind, the heat started skyrocketing. It felt like opening an oven door.

After the wind and the heat came the hills. Though they weren't as bad as Monarch pass, they were more frequent, difficult to climb, and made more challenging by the blistering air. My legs felt completely dead. In fact, I had to stop at points; a couple times, I ended up pushing my bike up the hills, feeling utterly defeated. So much so, I contemplated tenting on the side of the road. I'd like to say some altruistic motive kept me from quitting, but honestly, I didn't want to stop—simply because I was hungry and had no more food.

I pushed forward and found a lodge with a restaurant a couple miles ahead. Unfortunately, the prices were too much, but I was at least able to get some water. I knew I only had 16 more miles to reach Moab. Like the Little Engine that Could, I told myself, "I think I can," as I got back on the road.

The Little Engine had a hill to climb. I might as well have had one. As soon as I started back down the road, the headwinds picked up. That was not the pick-me-up I wanted. As I drew closer to where I would turn towards the south, I felt relief that the wind would soon shift. I said a quick prayer, asking God to take the wind away, said "amen," and turned the corner.

The wind picked up and blew so hard I had to stop. Even then, I could barely stay on my feet. For nearly 10 minutes, I stood still, my feet planted on the pavement, bracing myself against the gust of wind and wondering what I should do. The answer seemed simple enough. I only had one option at this point: just keep pushing ahead. After a mile or two, the wind died down enough to let me make some decent forward progress. I toughed it up and started pedaling as hard as I could, feeling a new burst of energy I didn't have before. That energy carried me through to a campground in Moab, Utah.

My verse came back to me again, "I can do all this through [Christ] who gives me strength" (Php 4:13). I knew I could overcome obstacles, but I had to be tapped into God and His strength and His power to do it. The most amazing thing about pushing through the winds was another chance encounter. The wind had delayed my trip much later than I intended. It was after 9pm and the first three campgrounds I tried in Moab were closed and didn't have pay stations. When I reached the last campground, I knew I had no choice. I would just need to stay there and pay in the morning.

After the sun rose, I walked to the office to square away my bill. I met Alisha working at the desk. She asked me if I needed a vehicle pass; I just had to laugh at the mental image of hanging a vehicle tag from the rear view mirror on my sunglasses. I told her I was riding a bicycle across America. This opened all kinds of conversation. She was a Christian and had faith in Christ, but she was also facing a tough situation. She was in her early 30's and the mother of two boys. She was scheduled to have a surgery the next day … and she wasn't certain she would survive.

God's timing surprised me again. He put me there just before this big event in her life, maybe just for the chance to pray with her and encourage her. I assured her God had bigger plans for her life and was in control of every situation. After we prayed, she offered to take me fishing with her boys, Elton and Adger, but it started to rain. Instead, she took me back to their house, where I had the chance to meet her mom, Linda, and enjoy some delicious homemade tacos.

With her permission, I contacted the people who had been praying for me and asked them to pray for her and her surgery as well. I knew God would hear my prayer, but I felt better knowing another dozen or more people were praying too.

Leaving the next day was difficult. Part of it was due to the terrain: 25 miles of hills and headwinds. The other part was my mind being constantly on Alisha and her surgery. I prayed for her most of the morning and into the afternoon. Finally, about 2:00 that afternoon, Linda called me and let me know Alisha came through her surgery just fine—news I was overjoyed to hear. I passed the praise down the prayer chain, making sure we thanked God for answering our prayer. It hit me at that point that I really was on God's schedule. One day difference either way and I would have missed the chance to meet Alisha and her family.

The next day, I made it to an interesting feature in the Canyonlands of Utah. It was called "Hole n' The Rock": a home literally carved into the mountain. Back in the 1940's Albert and Gladys Christensen used dynamite and chisels to make this "hole"—a 4000 square foot home with 14 rooms—including a fireplace with a chimney. It took nearly forty years to complete, almost a quarter of which was spent removing the broken-up rocks. Albert died just before it was completely finished. To honor him, Gladys carved a bathtub into the rock by herself after his death. Albert was also an artist, and many of his paintings still hung around the home. I was amazed at what people could do when they set their mind to a difficult task.

Speaking of difficult tasks, I knew I had to get back on the road, but while I was sightseeing, the winds had picked up again. On top of that, I had wanted to go to Canyonlands National Park, but I knew the road was entirely too difficult to make another detour. Discretion being the better part of valor, I decided to thumb a ride and see if someone could help me through the more treacherous parts of the trip. Brad and his truck responded and he offered to give me a ride. He sheepishly asked if we could take a small detour though... through the Canyonlands National Park! I was able to see the amazing striped mountains I had wanted to see and had a ride through in the process.

Brad actually dropped me off at the mountain top, allowing me to coast the 5 downhill miles to Monticello. I stayed there that night, having heard from Katie and Cheney that they were not too far away from where I was. With our paths so close to crossing, we decided to try and see if we could meet up somewhere.

I thought about homes and hospitality. In Acts 2 in the Bible, the young church had been growing by leaps and bounds. Luke wrote, "And all those who had believed were together and had all things in common; and they began selling their property and possessions and were sharing them with all, as anyone might have need" (Acts 2:44–45 NASB). I thought this was an amazing model of how the church should be. The funny thing is that it doesn't work if people force hospitality, but if they let it happen, great things come from it. I saw this with the Warm Showers people I had stayed with. When one receives hospitality, he or she knows what it's like and can return it. Even though I was taking a lot of hospitality from people, I thanked God when I had a chance to give back: buying a lunch, praying for Alisha, and making future plans to change my way of thinking.

At the root of hospitality is the idea of a home. The early church actually met in people's homes. And homes are at the center of who we are. I missed my home during this trip—having familiar things that represent who I am. But at the same time, I got to share in other people's lives. Whether it was Alisha taking me into her home and giving me a snapshot of her life, Brad bringing me into his truck, or seeing the work the Christensens had done on their rock home, I had a chance to be part of these people's lives—if only for a moment.

Churches now are all about the building. They have drives to raise funds and build bigger and better buildings. I started to think that churches needed to not focus on that so much. Church is about the people who bear Christ's name. When we meet in homes, we see people for who they are—not for who they pretend to be for a few hours on Sunday. It lets us see the pains, hurts, and the joys in their lives. God was certainly using this trip to change my perspective.

18: HIDDEN BEAUTY

Katie and Cheney decided to meet me, but as I was waiting for them, they called again and said they had been delayed—they left their identification behind and had to backtrack to get it. They were trying to hitch a ride to save some time. As much as I wanted to move on with my journey, I also couldn't wait to see them again! They were great company and always helped push me to be a better rider. It also was comforting to have people traveling together. I remembered the old buddy system in grade school and how we helped hold each other accountable ... long before we could ever spell accountability.

The Bible talks about that exact thing. "As iron sharpens iron, so one person sharpens another" Proverbs 27:17 NIV. When two people get together with the same goal in mind, they just make each other better. Even though there might be friction—and maybe even sparks—it all works for the greater good.

While I waited for Katie and Cheney, I used my iPhone to watch a movie on YouTube. Of all the movies, I could have picked, I found *127 Hours* a docu-drama about Aron Ralston, a man who had been hiking in the Canyonlands in 2003. Aron had suffered an accident that pinned his arm between the canyon wall and an 800 lb boulder. After five days of exposure, he finally chose to amputate his arm with a dull multi-tool. He was rescued and lived to tell his tale (and have a pretty good movie made about it).

In retrospect, it probably wasn't the best movie to watch, since I was so close to the place he had been and could be in much the same situation. Still, I knew God was watching over me, and He had sent so many other people to do the same. That was part of the reason I looked forward to reuniting with Katie and Cheney—we could be there for each other.

It was strange having time just to sit and think. I realized I had been on the road for almost four months at this point. So much of my life had been spent on this trip that I hadn't thought about what I might do when I finished. Yet I knew I was getting close enough to start contemplating that exact point. I used my phone and looked up different bicycles, thinking I might try to train for some races when I got back. I heard about the Pelotonia, a ride in Columbus, OH, that would raise money for cancer research. I thought it was a great cause and would be a chance to be on the road again. I also found the Ironman Triathlon and thought that might make for an amazing challenge. It was a 112 mi bike race, sandwiched between a 2.4 mile swim and a 26.2 mile run.

Katie and Cheney finally made it and my day of rest ended. On Friday, September 2nd, we headed towards Blanding, UT—a difficult ride with virtually no cell phone service. That's where I found out Monarch Pass was not the roughest part of the trip. As we drew close to the Natural Bridges National Monument, we found a 2000 ft climb crammed into a 10 mile stretch—that was about 10 degrees of incline. Up to this point, the most we had tried was 6 degrees and that had been hard enough.

Fortunately an RV picked us up and helped us through the most difficult part of the climb. They dropped us off at the National Park where we stayed overnight, simply in awe of all the beauty around us. This section of the trip was definitely one of the most scenic ... but unfortunately also one of the most treacherous. Steep drop offs surrounded us and made sure we paid close attention to our surroundings. We stayed in Hanksville, UT, at Hite National Park by Lake Powell. It had some basic facilities—including a store to stock up on supplies. We even took the time to swim there. The lake was absolutely

Mike meets the sights of Utah

amazing in itself, but the surroundings made it even more beautiful. Cliffs, 300 to 400 feet high, surrounded us, making us feel enclosed and safe.

We met some more bikers as well; they offered to let us stay on their site for free. Adam and Christy Coppola were a newly married couple; they were biking to reach all 50 states in a single calendar year. They had started January 10th and were completely self-supported. In fact, they were even doing this ride for two different charities relating to bicycles. They were using their trip to help buy hand-cycles for wounded veterans and also people in developing countries.

They were really a remarkable couple who had such compassion for other people. This world has so much in the way of resources but so few people have them. It takes radical people like Adam and Christy to wake us up and realize God uses all kinds of people to spread compassion. Adam and Christy journaled their trip at www.giveabike.com.

By Sunday, September 4th, we were pushing towards Torrey, UT. That morning was one of the roughest. Mosquito bites dotted my skin—arms, legs, even my neck and face. Later, I broke yet another tent pole. I was also tired—mostly due to the all-night argument between my stomach and my dinner. Still, I wanted to push ahead; I told myself, "Mind over matter,"

Thankfully, most of the early ride had semi-flat roads and only small inclines with which I had to contend. Unfortunately, our last 15 miles were filled with more intense uphill stretches. We stopped at a gas station about two miles from Torrey. I immediately thought that might have been a mistake; I wasn't sure if I was going to be able to start the ride again. Exhausted and not feeling well, it took every ounce of strength to get back on my bike and push the pedal. I told God I needed His strength to overcome my weakness. Each push became a little easier. I learned how powerful it was when I combined my faith in God with the power of my thoughts.

That night we stayed in a campground with Wi-Fi; unfortunately they didn't give us the code. I walked around trying to figure out how to get it. Fortunately the second couple I asked had it. Having access to the Wi-Fi was nice, but better yet, the couple had some lasagna they shared with us. I was so aware of how good food tasted when we could find it. As we ate the lasagna, we sat around the camp and talked.

"So how are you planning on getting home," Katie asked me, "after you get to San Francisco?"

Honestly, I had thought about it many times over the course of the trip, but I didn't really have a good answer for her. I had spent this entire trip trusting God to provide, and I knew He would ... I just didn't know how.

"Do you think you can make it down to L.A.? I have family there and you can stay with them a couple of weeks at least. Maybe you can find a way to work and earn money for the plane ticket home?"

I had to smile. Everything was just falling into place. That's how God works. He takes care of everything.

The next day, all we had to cover was a 40-mile ride to Boulder, Utah. It should have been an easy ride, but once again, the horizontal distances were not the problem— the vertical ones were. We had to push ourselves up and over many hills. To make it more challenging, it wasn't one straight shot. Periodically, the road would dip downhill, just enough to make us think things were getting better, and then they would get tough again. My trailer and the weight behind me didn't make the climb easy. But I pushed through the pain, telling myself that, when it was all said and done, it was going to be well worth it. The harder days made the finish that much more appreciated. In fact, just reaching the summit of this portion of the climb was an amazing experience. We had ridden 23 miles uphill over the course of four and half hours. And, true to form, it took only 30 minutes to descend.

Unlike Monarch Pass, we did stop once. We had to stop—not just for the sake of rest, but also to take in the beauty around us. About 14 miles up the hill, the view was too incredible to miss. We could see out for miles and miles; the stretching mountains, thick fog, and wide countryside were truly breathtaking. I realized the world is such a beautiful place. So many times we are locked into whatever we see or hear in our immediate vicinity. All it takes is a little stroll to find something different. God made the planet with such diversity, not just in people, but also in geography.

Unfortunately there were also a diversity of dangers as well. We had planned on trying a 74-mile run towards Bryce Canyon. To get there we had to go through a long stretch of road known as The Hogsback—a phenomenally curvy road with dangerous drops off both sides—and no guard rails.

An all-too-common site through most of Colorado and Utah

At points, it was a 14.1 percent grade downhill—enough to let us coast to 40 miles per hour before growing nervous enough to start squeezing our brakes. And, as always, there had to be one more challenge. It started raining, making the terrain much more slippery.

Finally, the rain forced us to find shelter. This was a fall rain—cold, biting knives that cut right through us. We tried to hitch for almost thirty minutes and couldn't find anything. Once again, as soon as we gave up, someone stopped and gave us a ride. He was great company ... him and his two dogs. The best part was that they were going all the way through to Bryce Canyon, so we ended up making our destination despite all challenges trying to keep us away!

As he dropped us off at the gate, we realized God was not finished blessing us. We ran into a friend of Katie and Cheney's who took us through the tunnel into the park. And because we were in the vehicle, we were all able to get in for one price.

Words may not be able to describe the beauty of Bryce Canyon, but that didn't stop Mike from enjoying it.

We camped for the night and spent the next day sightseeing. We took a three mile hike ... on foot! It had been a while since I had walked that long. This particular area was known for its slot canyons—deep and narrow crevices formed by rushing waters. The sides look almost like the rushing water that formed them—flowing curves with deep horizontal lines etched into them. I took over a hundred pictures while we walked; the scenery was just too amazing to pass up—certainly a once-in-a-lifetime experience

Above: The Subway ... western United States Style
Below: More of the breathtaking scenery from Bryce National Park

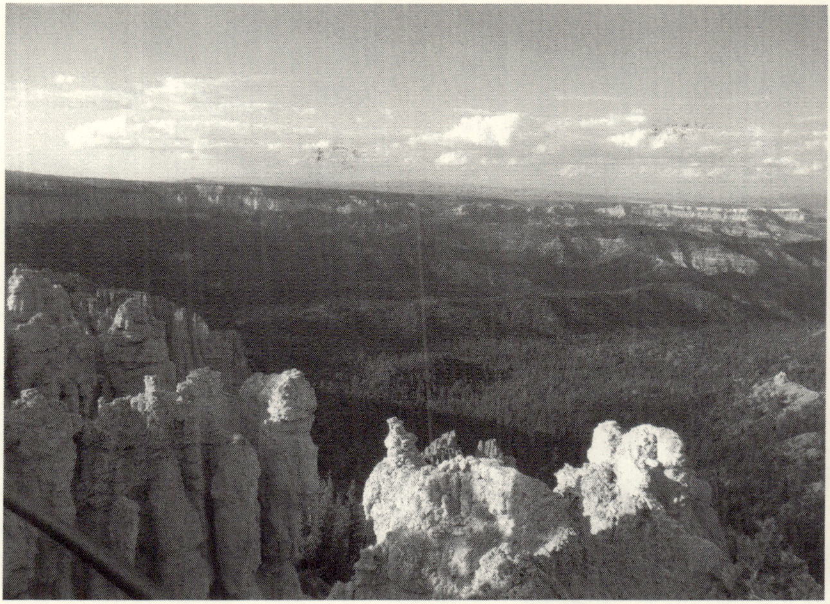

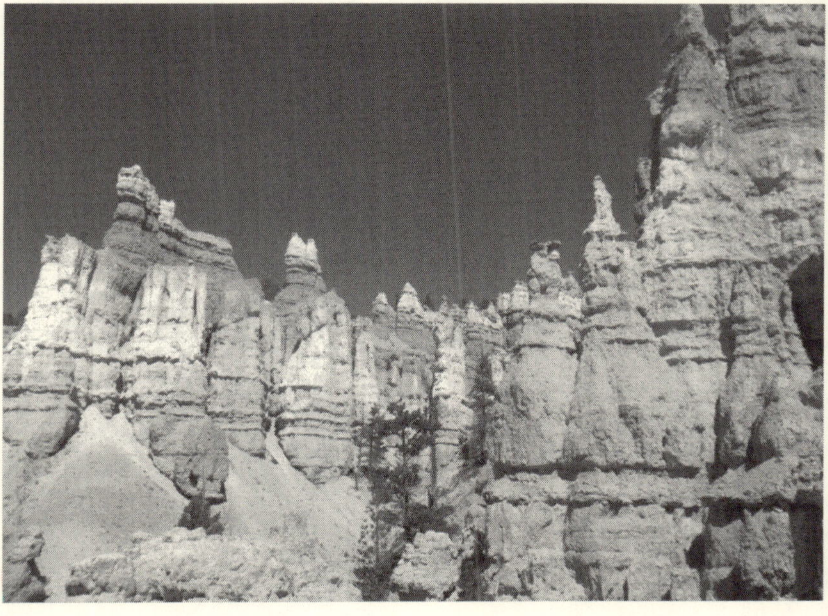

Interestingly, while we were there, we ran into Adam and Christy again! It turned out they were taking the same route as me through Nevada. I had planned on being alone through much of my trip and here I was with four other bicyclists! We all stayed together that night.

Instead of tenting in for the night though, I had the chance to enjoy the company we were sharing. Adam wanted to take a late-night hike to get some pictures of the stars. He was a photographer and the scenery out there was truly awesome. He invited me to join him and the two of us stayed out until 1am. Again and again, I just found myself in awe at the beautiful universe God had created. I had seen stars before, but not like that. We were away from all the city lights and pollution. I used to look up and try to count the stars; out here I just took them in. It would be impossible to count them all. It seemed like I could see farther than I ever did before, out to the edge of the Milky Way where the stars swirled like some cosmic river.

We left the next day and headed towards Hatch, UT, just a short 27 mile ride, most of which was downhill. We stopped and camped. I ate my peanut butter and jelly without complaining, though I was painfully aware I only had $2 left to my name. But I thought back to the stars from the previous night, and about the God who placed them all in the sky and created the amazing land masses back on the earth. That God still understood me—Mike Baker—and took time to answer my prayers. I said a quick prayer to that God, feeling myself fall back into the cycle of worry. It was hard to ignore my monetary worries, but I knew God was getting ready to bless me again.

On Friday, September 9th, we rode 60 miles towards Zion National Park in Utah. I rode quieter than normal. I knew I would be in trouble when we arrived at the park. Two dollars wouldn't get me a step past the gate. It took all my strength to swallow my pride and ask Katie and Cheney if they could cover my admission cost. They, of course, agreed quickly and wholeheartedly ... but they didn't have to. Adam and Christy had arrived before us and put us on their admission pass. And as if that wasn't enough, the campsites were all full, but someone had seen Adam and Christy and invited us all to stay with them. First I had been worrying about how I was going to pay to get in ... and suddenly I had free admission and a free campsite for a few days. God wasn't messing around!

Katie and Cheney as they hitch a ride into Zion National Park

This became a new pattern for us. At points of the trip, other cyclists would join us as well. Sometimes there was as many as eight of us together. We didn't all cycle together the whole time, but we knew we would see each other at various points. Adam and Christy had developed their own rhythm and woke up around 5 or 6 each morning to start their trip. Typically, they would ride ahead and we would catch up with them later, often staying at the same campgrounds.

Zion National Park was gorgeous. Cliffs stretched upwards all around us and deep gulches had been carved into the ground. We hiked all around the park—including an 8-mile round trip hike around Observation Point. In case it wasn't obvious, hiking in bike shoes is highly not recommended, but it was definitely worth it. At the top of Observation Point, we looked down and saw the amazing sights—the Virgin River valley that made everything lush and green while gigantic sandstone cliffs stretched upwards along both sides.

As we returned to camp, we shared food. Katie and Cheney gave me some of their pasta—which was a lot better than one of the two peanut butter and jelly sandwiches I had left. As we ate and talked together, other cyclists arrived and joined us. Eventually, eight of us sat together and told stories.

Eight random strangers coming together by sharing meals, stories, and companionship at Zion National Park

Sunday, we continued our rest at Zion by taking a shuttle to Angel's landing—one of the most famous hikes in the US. It's a long rock fin that's so dangerous the park installed poles with chains so hikers can hold onto them the entire way. Probably the best description for someone who has not seen it would be to liken it to a giant diving board overlooking the most wide open, deep canyon imaginable. It was definitely the best hike of the trip. I also had a chance to see another rare sight ... a tarantula! Things were definitely different out there.

The view from Angel's Landing

I tried my best to forget about my money situation but it always seemed to be in the forefront of my mind. Then I got a message from Tom stating he had put $40 in my account ... that would buy a ton more peanut butter and jelly sandwiches!

The next morning, I woke up to a wet tent; it was apparently leaking somewhere. I just counted it as joy and looked forward to what God had for me that day—a hike through one of the most famous slot canyons, known as The Subway. The park only gave out 60 permits a day, so they were in high demand. We had to hitchhike to get there in time, but we did. It was certainly worth it.

As we walked through the large curved chamber, we saw about every color known to man in the walls! Afterwards, we ended the day at the waterfalls and went swimming.

As I floated in the clear water, I thought about those people who never left the comfort of their own homes and would never get to experience some of what I did. I thought about people I know who had never left central Ohio and were perfectly content being there their whole lives. I think their biggest problem is fear. People are too afraid of what will happen if they leave their comfort zones. They could be injured, lost, or something worse could happen to them. And while I understand being afraid, I would encourage people to go for it, or they will miss out on some amazing things. I had travelled enough to know there are some beautiful places in America, but nothing compared with the sights of Zion National Park and the other places I visited. If I hadn't taken a risk and set out on my bike, I would never have seen Observation Point, Angel's Landing, or The Subway. Could something bad happen to me? Of course! Aron Ralston and his self-amputated arm showed me that. For me, the key is faith. Faith and fear are really just two sides of the same coin. Fear is having faith that something bad is going to happen. Faith expects good things to happen. I for one, chose to be a man of faith!

Cheney, Katie, Mike, Adam ... & Christy behind the camera

The sights of Zion National Park

Hidden Beauty

19 VIGNETTE: MEET THE PARENTS
PHIL, SR. & LILA BAKER

As Mike walked out onto Angel's Landing and turned to wave at Adam holding his camera, he had no clue what his parents would think when they saw the video.

"Mikey, get away from the edge!" yelled Phil Baker, Sr., knowing the unpredictable Utah winds. Mike, almost 6000 miles away certainly could not hear his father, but the man communicated his point well—especially to Mike's mother, Lila, as she held the iPhone that played the video.

The scene had become somewhat normal at the Tuesday night Bible study the Baker's attended. Phil was a self-admitted "cave-man" when it came to technology. He used an old flip phone. "I can type four words per minute with about 80 mistakes," he said. Yet, he embraced the technology that would allow him to keep up with his youngest son's travels.

He didn't follow too closely, though. He worried about his boy being on the road, but also knew that what he didn't know wouldn't scare him. He never even found out about the truck that hit Mike until after the trip. He said if he had known that, he would have worried more. Mike knew that as well, which was why he omitted the detail until after the trip was completely finished.

The bottom line is that behind every good man ... is a great set of parents. While some people may read Mike's book and wonder *How in the world does one person have the faith to take on such an incredible feat?* others may look at it and wonder *How in the world do parents sit by and let their children take off across the country with virtually nothing to their name?*

Phil and Lila Baker of Johnstown, Ohio did just that. Though truthfully, they had little choice in the matter. Mike gave them very little warning—not quite a week. They were hard-pressed to discourage Mike from going. Phil, who describes his youngest son as being his free-spirited one, was quick to point out that at the same age Mike embarked on his trip, he had already been married four years and had two sons.

The Bakers tried to help with the preparations— Phil made sure to tell Mike to travel light. The possessions would slow him down. Underneath their calm exteriors though, the trip left them with mixed emotions. On one hand, they were happy he was undertaking such a daunting task, especially with the purpose of growing his faith.

On the other hand, they were apprehensive for sure—even worried at times. But said they were not petrified—though they did pray for him every night. The biggest challenge for them came when Mike couldn't find a place to stay. "There's all these stories of serial killers and all these freaks out there—we worried about that. Our baby was taking off into vast unknowns."

Mike was the Baker's baby—the youngest of four boys ... though that also meant he had three older brothers to help toughen him up. All the brothers are quite unique and have chosen their own routes in life. His next oldest brother was Tom. Phil described him as the prodigal, who became an ordained minister. The next oldest was Guy: with his Master's degree in criminology, he was in charge of the Loss Prevention of Victoria's Secret outlet stores. The oldest was Phil Jr. - who owned his own basement remodeling company.

Phil loves his sons and says he is proud—and blessed—for the way they have turned out. "I think they get it from me being self-employed—they are not afraid to try anything." That sense of fearlessness and invincibility is a family trait. Phil always tried to teach his boys, "If you think you can do it, you can do it."

141 Days: Bike for Christ

"They're all successful," Phil said. "They get up every morning thinking they can do anything."

In some aspects, the Bakers faced as great of a challenge as Michael. As the biking Baker was traveling across the country, his parents were facing their own challenges. They were going through some fairly serious financial problems at the time and could not help Mike out as much as they would have liked. Just like Mike, they were forced to rely on the kindness of strangers and on their faith for Mike's provisions.

This didn't change their opinion of the trip. "I'm glad he did this trip," Phil said—and then quickly added, "I'm glad it's over." He said it was something that is good to do when people are young and don't have attachments holding them down.

Of course that didn't stop the Bakers. They live out the missions mentality in their own lives. Once they went to the Bowery Mission in New York City. Phil said he went out there on his "high horse," thinking he was going to serve the people there. "Instead, they ended up serving me," he said. "Here were these people who were happy just to have a meal and a place to stay. They still had faith, even though they had nothing else. Sometimes we worry about what we need—or what we think we need—and then you go someplace like that and get taught a lesson from someone who has absolutely nothing."

One of Phil's favorite scripture passages is Luke 10, The Parable of the Good Samaritan. Laced with cultural nuances, the main thrust of the story follows a man who is robbed and beaten almost to the point of death. Two of the leading religious figures passed him by for whatever their own reasons might have been. Then help came from an unlikely source—the title character of the good Samaritan. Once again, the culturally-rejected becomes the hero. He gave the victim first aid, took him to an inn, and even paid for medical care, going above and beyond anything the people could imagine.

The traveler, much like Mike, was someone's son. He had a mother and father, who—for whatever reason—were not there with him at the same time. And Mike, like the traveler, was taken in and cared for by not just one, but countless numbers of people on his way across the United States. The parable was acted out again, again, and again in Mike's story. Like their trip to the Bowery Mission, Mike's journey strengthened his parent's faith as much as it did his own.

The closer Mike got to his goal, the more his parents worried about one final challenge. How would they get him home from California? That miracle would have to wait.

20: THE LONELIEST ROAD IN AMERICA

Leaving Mt. Zion was difficult to the point of being painful. Along with the breathtaking scenery, I had also grown accustomed to having a lot of people around again. Eight cyclists together seemed like a huge crowd after so many days spent on my own. I had known it wouldn't last forever, though. As we left Zion, Katie and Cheney turned southwest towards Las Vegas to continue on to Los Angeles.

Fortunately, I still had Adam and Christy to keep me company. On the 13th of September, we had only a couple hundred miles left of Utah and then we would be hitting Route 50 in Nevada—dubbed the "Loneliest Road in America" for its long flat desert terrain, uninterrupted by houses and stores. I felt a little trepidation, but determined to make the best of the last couple days I had on this side of it.

We tried to find a Warm Shower host in Cedar City, Utah, but she never answered her phone. While we were figuring out what to do, we looked up and saw the sky looked like rain. We had learned something from our time out west—when it looked like rain, we wanted to find shelter quickly. Storms could move fast out there. We headed towards a Wal-Mart and, just as we arrived, it started to rain. We took advantage of the break to buy some supplies. I stocked up on more peanut butter and jelly, leaving me with only $6 to my name as I left the store.

Adam and Mike hide from the rain in Wal-Mart ... and have fun in the process

Instead of forcing our way through rain, we headed towards a Starbucks and decided to wait it out there. While we took shelter, we started a conversation with Bob and Nancy. They were a great couple and it was nice to share stories and pass the time. They also blessed us highly, buying us apple turnovers while we waited.

Then, as he was leaving, Bob dropped two bills in our laps. "Buy some energy bars," he told us.

It wasn't until he and Nancy left that we looked at what he had given us: Bob had just handed us $100 for energy bars. We split the money, laughing with joy.

Mike, Adam, Bob, and Nancy finding shelter from the rain

"Does that sort of thing always happen to you?" Adam asked me.

I laughed and said "Yeah, actually it does. Praise the Lord!" I was still amazed though. Again, words really can't convey how much things like that meant to me. The money Bob handed me was almost 10 times as much as I had. It would feed me for quite some time.

By dinner time, the rain had finally subsided. We knew the day was pretty well shot and we were going to have to find a place to stay. I called a number of churches, but no one was available to help. There was a KOA campground close by, but I really didn't want to go to it. First, even with Bob and Nancy's blessing, I still didn't have a great deal of money. KOA's, though they are a great chain of campgrounds, they tended to be a little higher priced than I had budgeted and I still was trying to save money. Second, it was four miles out of the way. So I picked a different road for us to see what we could find, figuring if there was nothing down that way, we could always head back to the KOA.

Instead, we found a church. I laughed and told Adam and Christy this place would hook us up with the hospitality we needed. "I bet we get a place to stay here," I said. Indeed, the church just happened to be holding a cookout. Everyone seemed like they were having a great time and, when they saw us, they invited us for dinner and offered to let us stay on the property for the night.

Fortunately the church members also had some foresight to go with their generosity. Someone remembered the sprinklers started automatically at night—which would have been an unwelcome surprise. A man named Enoch offered to let us stay at his place instead. Just to show how much God loves dealing with the details, I had really wanted a tree to stay under since my tent had been leaking so badly ... and of course, Enoch's land had several of them from which I could choose. His garage even had a place for us to shower.

Their generosity amazed me. While we pitched out tents, one of the men from the church came by and dropped off a bag of apples, oranges, and bananas. It had been quite some time since we had fresh fruit. He also dropped off a copy of the Book of Mormon for us! I guess I hadn't paid attention to what type of church it was. It was interesting that when people are in need, differences don't matter. Human beings are human beings and we needed help regardless of what our beliefs might be.

It made me think about when Jesus said to love our neighbor as ourselves. He didn't put any contingencies on it. He didn't say to love the neighbors we love ... or love the ones who look and act like we do ... or love the ones who smell good.

In fact, I love the passage in John 4 where Jesus talks to a Samaritan woman at a well. As I understand it, the

Samaritans and Jews didn't see eye to eye on a lot of things. The Jews would even walk around Samaria just to avoid the people there. Yet, Jesus and His disciples marched right up the middle of the area. In the middle of the day, when the sun was at its hottest (and I really started to understand that concept during this trip) He stood by the town well and met a woman who didn't have the best of reputations. Yet He still took the time to hold a conversation with her—even though His own disciples didn't understand what He was doing.

The next day was a nice 55 mile ride for us: small climbs with nice downhill stretches. We were still approaching the Loneliest Road, but we were not there yet. We had no plans for a place to stay, but we figured something would present itself. We arrived in Milford, UT, about 3:30 in the afternoon and stopped for a refreshment break. I had been craving a Dr. Pepper, and while we were at the store, we found Clark. He asked us about our trip and we shared with him who we were and what we were doing. He asked us where we were planning on staying.

"Probably a campsite," Adam said.

"Well it's going to rain, so I'm not going to let you do that," Clark said. "You're coming to my house for beds and dinner. Then I'll cook you pancakes and eggs."

On the way to Clark's house, Mike and Adam have one small series of hurdles to overcome as they carry their gear over some railroad tracks

True to his word, Clark took all three of us to his place, cooked us pasta and salad for dinner, and gave us ice cream and apple turnovers for desert. That night, we all shared stories in between taking showers and doing laundry. And God was continuing to look out for me; I received word my grandfather had given me $100 to help out with my trip.

On Thursday, September 15th, we said goodbye to Clark and started onto Route 50 through Nevada. "The Loneliest Road in America" lay before us: 84 miles of road through the desert with no services. "No services"

in this area meant almost no buildings and nothing but desert.

Clark told us that around the halfway point of the trip there would be a vacant building that still served as a water supply. We knew we could at least fill up our packs there. Even if the water wasn't perfect, it would still be okay. Adam and Christy had a water purifier called a Steripen to allow them to drink any water they wanted. They could literally pull water out of a swamp and the purifier would kill all the bacteria.

There would be no turning back and no stopping once we started down that road. I was glad I had Adam and Christy with me. We were definitely a "cord of three strands" and we could be there to help one another. We pushed each other through the ride, adjusting to the Nevadan terrain. It wasn't flat like I had expected; it was a series of small hills—climb ... flat ... climb ... flat. The climbs in the desert heat seemed to just suck the life out of me. We pushed through them, counting down the miles as we rode along. It was a brutal stretch of road— there wasn't even any shelter to hide from the sun and heat ... not that we wanted to stop.

Adam and Mike shelter themselves for a brief rest along Rt. 50

As I continued to press onward, I felt my CamelBak getting lighter. It made me nervous as I knew the water reserves on my trailer were gone. Fortunately, about 40 miles into the ride, we came upon the building Clark had told us about. We started looking around to find the water source and had no luck. A truck pulled in and the driver asked us what we were doing.

"Looking for the water," I said.

"There's no water there," he told us. Apparently, the building had been vacant for some time.

That was not the news we wanted to hear with over another 40 miles of desert ahead of us. The man did have a cooler and offered us each a soda or a CapriSun. It wasn't much, but we couldn't turn it down. I just tried to keep my eyes on God and remember He was going to take care of us. I knew He would protect me, but this was another one of the times I started to get a little nervous about His timing. The exhaustion was breaking down my body. I couldn't push myself as hard; I watched Adam and Christy pull ahead so far that I couldn't see them over the small inclines.

And that's where it happened: on the "Loneliest Road in America" two ATV Gators zipped right past me—too quickly for me to stop them and ask them for water and yet slowly enough I could clearly see a cooler strapped to the back of the second one.

I just started praying that Adam and Christy would be able to stop them and that they would offer us some water. As I crested the peak of the hill, I saw Adam and Christy ... and the Gators and their riders. I sighed in relief as I pedaled towards them.

As we talked and shared stories, I had to laugh at the situation. They were out enjoying the desert heat that had been so brutal to us. Their situation was so different— they were carrying several coolers with them and had everything anyone could have needed: water, snacks, pop, and more food!

On the Loneliest Highway, God had somehow provided us with a mobile refreshment stand.

As we were talking with them, a motorcyclist who had

been driving the opposite direction pulled over just to say hi. We were surprised to see him again, because we had met him a couple of days prior at a gas station. Doug had asked us if we had run into his son—who was traveling across the country on a bicycle as well; he was trying to surprise him and meet up with him. We hadn't seen Doug's son, but that didn't stop him from handing us each a bottle of water, a Gatorade, and a bag of delicious cookies.

The Gators, Doug, and us cyclists all went our separate ways, but it wasn't more than a minute later that the Gators had turned around and stopped us again. They apologized for interrupting our ride and handed us $60 so we could have a nice dinner! We had to laugh. Their "interruption" probably saved our lives, and having money for a nice meal made things even better. This certainly didn't seem like "The Loneliest Road in America" to us.

This is what "The Loneliest Road in America" looks like to Mike Baker

Having survived that ordeal, we stayed in Baker, Nevada—which I can't say I minded at all. The name indicated it was probably a pretty nice place! The following day we planned on trying 62 miles to Ely, NV: two big climbs with flat ground between them. We finished our first climb and took a short break. As we did, we watched a storm coming in and knew this one was going to be bad. The entire valley turned smoky from the rain as it rushed towards us. I wish I could describe the scene adequately. In literally five minutes, the day went from being perfectly clear to not being able to see more than 50 feet in front of us—pelted by driving rains, and trying to stand upright against gusting winds.

We put on our rain gear. Pedaling slowly through low visibility, we pushed ahead, hoping to find a safe haven from the storms. After the lightning and thunder started, we realized we really needed to find shelter soon. It wasn't just about convenience and comfort anymore; this was a life-threatening situation. There was only one house anywhere close by, so we headed towards it. We knocked several times, but received no answer so we took shelter under an overhang behind the house while the storm raged around us.

About 10 minutes later, Adam walked around front to grab something from his bike and realized the home owner had arrived. He opened the door and asked Adam what we were doing on his property. Adam, as politely as he could, explained we had come to him seeking shelter from the storm. The man, quite rudely and abrasively, asked us if we understood the concept of private property.

"I'm sorry," Adam apologized. "Do you want us to leave?"

We certainly didn't want to have to go back into the storm and figured the man would be nice enough to let us at least stand under his overhang while waiting for the rain, thunder, and lightning to diminish. Who would send three travelers back into the rain?

That guy would.

"Yes!" he said, answering Adam's spoken question and my silent one in one fell swoop.

As we headed back into the elements, the man continued to yell at us, telling us it was our generation that started disrespecting people's privacy. I've never witnessed such an awful situation. He certainly had the right to do what he did. We were on his property, but we had not asked much of him—just a dry place in a dangerous situation.

It was such a stark contrast to the generosity I had experienced, but it served as a gigantic reminder. The blessings on this trip had come from God. Human nature is naturally selfish and defensive. It takes something special to push us out of the natural state. I thought about him and felt sorry for him. I figured it was possible that, for whatever reason, he had never been shown love, or something had hurt him to make him that angry.

Of course, most of those philosophical thoughts came after the fact. The immediate concern was to fight through the cold, driving rain and find another place for shelter. With our hands and feet soaked and starting to go numb, we began the second climb of the day. Near the top of the climb, we found a cafe. We didn't even need to ask each other—we were going to stop there. As our exhausted legs drug our soaking feet into the cafe, we encountered two more cyclists. They introduced themselves as Jesse and Royal—it turned out that Royal was Doug's son! We enjoyed the rest and the company for about an hour—then the rain stopped and the sun came out.

We hit the road again, finishing the last five miles and then enjoying a long descent towards Ely, Nevada. As we got close to town, the sky began to threaten rain again. We knew we couldn't do another run in the rain like we had, so we chose to split a motel room between the three of us. Although it continued to pour rain, we got to stay safe and dry!

The next day we headed towards Eureka, Nevada, continuing our trek through the Loneliest Road. We faced four mountain passes to climb, probably over 4000 feet in elevation. It took every bit of energy, which unfortunately wasn't much after the previous day. The cold weather and strain of the trek had taken their toll on my legs. As we pushed our way through the passes, each one became progressively more difficult. To complicate things, the weather had started growing colder. Between the elevation and tipping the balance of September towards October, the heat certainly was no longer my only challenge ... the cold was becoming one too. The nights were certainly the worst; the cold made it so difficult to sleep.

I don't know what I would have done without Adam and Christy there; they made it much more bearable. Even during my video recording, they loved to ham it up. Once, they took my phone and did the update for me. And it wasn't uncommon to see Adam jumping into the frame and yelling, "Hi mom." Sometimes a sense of humor is the most important thing someone can take with them on a trip. Moments of laughter always helped me forget about some of the more dire circumstances I couldn't change. Instead, I was just able to rejoice in the moment.

After reaching Eureka, we fought three more passes through to Austin, Nevada. That night we stayed at a Baptist church campground that gave us half off our stay. As I tried to bunk down for the night, I tossed and turned, feeling a sore throat coming on. I prayed quickly and had others pray for me. Fortunately the tightness in my throat was gone by the next morning, though I still felt a little sick. We pushed on towards Cold Springs and then Fallon, Nevada. The closer I drew to the California border, the more I realized how different life was going to be. Of course I had one more obstacle to overcome: I still had to get home. Thanks to some of the blessings that had rolled in, I had $160.00. That was enough to feed me and to find a place to stay for a couple nights, but it was a far cry from a plane ticket home—and that was just for me; it didn't even include trying to get my bike and my other gear home.

Even more than that, I realized that life was going to take another humongous change. My life on the road had become a new "Rutyna Zabicia." My responsibilities had been only to me. Even though God had provided traveling companions, we were still all somewhat alone ... or self-sufficient at least. And while it had been an amazing time, it would inevitably come to an end. The good news was I had a ton of ideas for things that could change when I arrived home. I had started to become a little more comfortable speaking in front of groups, so I wanted to try my hand at some public speaking. I thought it would be amazing to share the things God had put in my heart. I also had all the ideas God had given me for church, though I had no clue how to see them come to pass. And that led my mind to the greatest challenge:

when I got home the rubber was going to hit the road—
ironically.

Above: Rt. 50 - The Loneliest Road in America   *Photo Courtesy of Coppola Photography*

21 VIGNETTE - ADAM AND CHRISTY COPPOLA
www.GiveaBike.com and
www.coppolaphotography.com

One cannot spend more than three minutes on Adam and Christy's website without cracking up with laughter. There are pictures of Adam and Mike holding Christy on their shoulders in front of the Nevada border sign, Christy holding Adam's bicycle shorts that had to be mailed to him when he left them behind at a campsite (thankfully, he had another pair), and an incredibly liberal interpretation of the street sign reading "Twin Buttes." The string of blog entries are just as amusing as the pictures. For instance, after their trial run of the bike tour, Christy wrote the following summary:

1. Training is a must. It will not be any easy thing to bike 65 miles a day and our 3 training rides of 25 miles just didn't cut it.
2. $40 per day will be tough to stick to.
3. Adam can eat 3 full meals after a day of biking
4. $40 per day will be impossible if Adam always eats like that!

Of course there is more to them than humor. The Coppola's website is full of breath-taking photos from every type of geography: waterfalls, cliffs, slot canyons, and - of course - the open road. They also have collections of photos from the many different people they met along the way.

Adam and Christy had been married only a few months before the trip started. Christy was working as a teacher and Adam was on the track to being a school counselor. They had talked about doing something significant—thinking of the Peace Corps or some other such venture. That conversation turned into a series of scribbles on the back of a sushi restaurant placemat. The next thing Adam and Christy knew, they were telling their parents their plans to raise money for two charities by biking to all 50 states in a year.

Their parents had mixed reactions. Christy said her parents are more of the easygoing, free-spirited, go-with-the-wind type. They thought if Adam and Christy had their hearts set on the journey, they should go for it. Adam said his parents had the opposite reaction. "They were more like, 'What are you talking about? You went to college. You went to grad school. Now you're supposed to get a job." They thought Adam needed to have a life-plan in place and didn't see the benefit of bicycling for a year. They changed their minds as the trip progressed. "That was the most rewarding part," Adam said. "They changed and became our biggest supporters and we could see their happiness and pride."

The Coppola's left Monday, January 10th, 2011, flying to San Diego, CA. According to their website, "Their focus is on charity, adventure, and physical challenge, all visible through photography, videography, and journalistic blogging." Those goals meant that Adam and Christy had to carry some serious gear with them—including an iPhone, iPad, and a small laptop as well as Adam's camera and four lenses. They also had a portable battery to charge their electronics. In addition, they carried many of the same basics as Mike did: a tent, bike tools, and sleeping bags. Adam and Christy also brought a camping stove, a pot, extra food—including an emergency meal, a water filter, sleeping bags, and some mace for protection. They carried a limited amount of clothing—two biking outfits and one off-the-bike one. Adam and Christy had also brought a SPOT satellite messenger (www.findmespot.com), that served several purposes for them. First, it had an emergency 911-type button that they could press if things ever became difficult. It would transmit their distress signal and location to the authorities. It also had a breakdown feature which is, as they described, AAA for adventurers. If they were okay physically but needed help, they could press that one. The feature they used most often was the "I'm okay" button. At the end of their daily ride, they would press that button and it would send an email to everyone they had selected. The email would state their location and a short message to tell people they were safe. They didn't have to call a list of people every night, and still their families knew they were safe.

Aside from their families, Adam and Christy had other supporters as well. They had numerous people who sponsored them along the way. When they began the trip, they knew they didn't have enough money to finish it, but they were trusting that something would come along and help them finish. Indeed, they were able to keep on budget and finish their trip together.

In addition to the sponsorship for the trip, Adam and Christy also worked at helping to raise money for charities. Seventy percent of their proceeds went to

World Bicycle Relief (http://www.worldbicycle relief.org) to provide bikes for people in developing countries. Thirty percent of their trip went to Achilles International (http://www.achillesinternational.org/) and Freedom Team of Wounded Vets (http://www.achillesinternational.org/programs/free dom-team/overview) to raise money for hand-cycles, allowing veterans who lost a limb the ability to ride. To help raise this money, they did 35 different talks—sharing their story at bike shops, schools, outdoors clubs, and anyone else who would listen.

Mike definitely had an impact on their trip. They had met him through Katie and Cheney, a couple with whom they had run into periodically and would stay with in the evenings.

"At first it was just casual conversation," Adam said. "We were on different schedules. Christy and I had eaten and finished getting ready for bed when they rolled in."

They all ran into each other a few nights later at Bryce Canyon. "We were on the same schedule that night," Adam said. "Someone had recommended that we take a night hike. I wanted someone to go with me, but no one wanted to … except Mike."

Christy said, "I was thrilled to have Mike around because that meant I didn't have to go. I was quite happy."

By the time Adam and Christy met Mike, they

had already been on the road for nine months. At first Christy was apprehensive about having other riders around, wondering what effect it would have on their routine. Later, she realized that thought was—as she put it—"stupid." People didn't need to be together every minute. They could hook up at different stops and rest areas and share stories, food, and companionship. Christy said that was one of the best parts of the trip.

One of the benefits of companionship was along that Loneliest Road in America. They had already been through Iowa and were used to long stretches of road with little in the way of services. They feared Highway 50 would be the same monotony as Iowa but with even less civilization. Yet, with Mike with them, it was an entirely different experience.

They both loved Mike's companionship. They were amazed at his stories of God's blessings—the new bike, the chance encounters, and all the provision he had been given. Even more so, they enjoyed his personality.

"You only have to spend a few minutes with Mike to know that he's always smiling and always positive." Adam said. "We'd have a worry, like where we were going to find our next water. Next thing we know two ATV's roll up in the middle of nowhere. What the heck? Then they take off, come back, and give us money for dinner! Things like that always happened with Mike around." Adam said he could easily recount five different stories along that line.

One of Adam's favorite stories about Mike was the story of Pancake. During one of their rest stops, Mike had a leaf bug on his shoulder. "Normal people would flick it off or brush it away. Not Mike. He picks up and puts it on his bike and says, 'I think I'll call him Pancake.'"

Pancake the leaf bug joining the trip to San Francisco

Adam and Christy made a bet on how long Pancake would ride on Mike's handlebars, guessing a mile or two at most. Pancake ended up being part of a cross-country bicycle tour for nine or ten miles.

Christy said that was the fun of having Mike around. "There wasn't any monotony with him. We were having a blast."

Mike had such an impression on Adam and

Christy that a month or two after they went separate
ways they still thought and talked about him. At one
point, a ladybug landed on Adam's arm. Instead of
flicking it off, Adam took a picture of it and sent it to
Michael with the caption, "I think I'll name him
Flapjack."

Living on the road meant being creative and Mike
helped bring some of the fun. But they also helped each
other. "We ate a little better than Mike," Christy said
in reference to the peanut butter and jelly sandwiches
Mike seemed to always be eating. "We kept trying to
give him more food but he wouldn't always take it."
Adam and Christy had grown accustomed to their own
routine of food. "We would eat oatmeal in the
morning," Christy said, "a tuna fish wrap in the
afternoon, and our evening meal was always some
combination of pasta, meat, and vegetables in a pot."
Routine is not always a negative thing. Adam and
Christy said the food was awesome every night. "We
have never enjoyed food that much—everything we
ate was the best thing we had eaten," Christy said.

The food was one challenge in taking such a
massive trip. Adam and Christy faced many more—
probably nothing more challenging than the weather.
Since their trip spanned from January to November,
they faced all seasons and weather patterns. They
biked through blizzards, severe cold, two weeks of
pouring rain in the northeast, and even a tornado sixty

miles from them. They both agreed that the scariest moment was a thunderstorm that seemed to be right on top of their tent. It shook them up for a while and they found themselves not wanting to push through when severe weather hit around them.

They faced other obstacles as well. With the variety in locations, dangerous animals would be inevitable. Christy said that amongst the wildlife, the worst problem they had was with squirrels. At their camp in Zion, she came across the fattest squirrels she'd ever seen—they'd eat any food they could find. They also had encountered marshmallow-stealing raccoons. When they were camping with a family—a mother and father traveling with their four year old—the raccoon took the whole bag and ran off into the woods.

Times of adversity made Adam and Christy appreciate each other more. They kept each other going. When one would question their resolve on the trip and want to quit, the other would help.

"The one rule we had," Adam said, "we had right from the beginning: if the trip gets in the way of us and the relationship, it's over."

Christy said they didn't have to worry about that. "If anything, it made it that much stronger." She said that they had nothing to rely on but each other. Even though they had met tons of people and had so much support, it still boiled down to just them at the end of the day. They learned a great deal about each other.

"The tent can get smelly," Adam said, in his typically joking manner.

Adam and Christy certainly had a sense of humor in the way they teased each other. They started their trip in California and ended in Hawaii. Between those stops, Adam would tease his wife: "If it wasn't for Christy's bladder, we'd be in Hawaii."

Christy was quick to jab back, "Yes, but with Adam's navigational skills, we might still be in CA."

They also found humor in their situations. For instance, when they were north of Lake Tahoe, Adam hung his bike shorts out overnight. The next morning, they were nowhere to be found."

"He's fairly certain there's a bear out there wearing his bike shorts," Christy said.

Overall, the trip—including and especially their time with Mike—was an incredible adventure for Adam and Christy. They said they probably will not do something as huge as the year long trip again, but they are certainly up to week and month long excursions.

"We still have a sense of adventure," Adam said. "We just find a different way to do it." Adam said they will always do things unconventionally—it's part of who they are. "We have unconventional jobs and want to continue to do so."

While the Give a Bike organization is still open,

it's not active. However, the World Bicycle Relief and Achilles International Charity are still in need. In fact, when people contact the organizations and want to do larger projects, they often refer the people to Adam and Christy. The couple helps them plan their trip and gives advice where needed.

Adam said, "We get calls from people who want to go to all the national parks in the United States, or visit the highest point of every state, or visit local farms." They even received a call from a couple in their 60's who wanted to undertake a similar trip.

Adam and Christy both have the same advice to someone who wants to undertake such an adventure: "Do it." Adam added, "The hardest part is making the decision and going through with it. But if you really want to do it, do it. Don't let things hold you back." Indeed, Adam leaving his photography business and Christy resigning from her teaching position were both difficult decisions, but they agree that it was well-worth it in the long run.

"I thought the national parks would be the best part," Christy said, "but it was the people." Both of them were blown away by the generosity of those whom they met, whether it was through the Warm Showers, their friends and family, or their relatively brief encounter with Mike Baker.

22: THE JOURNEY HOME

On September 22, after a breakfast at McDonald's, I parted ways with the last of my traveling companions, Adam and Christy ... twice. I actually left once, but then I realized I had left my phone charger behind at the restaurant. While they brought it to me, I looked at the maps and realized I was only 317 miles from San Francisco.

This is where my story started: Carson City, Nevada at 2:00pm. I sold my trailer and shipped my tent, sleeping bag, and most of my other supplies back home. I had already found out I could travel faster unencumbered.

Twenty miles later, I reached the California border and faced 20 miles of a 4000 ft climb. I made the first five miles as the sun descended. It dropped quickly and plunged me into a darkness I had not expected. It was a completely different experience climbing a lonely pitch black road in the middle of the night by myself. After a brief rest, I continued on my way but only made it a few more miles before I needed to stop. I found the "closed for the season" campground, and laid next to the outhouse to try to shelter myself against the wind. I tried to sleep a little but couldn't, so I got back on the road again. About 3:30 am I found a lodge with an indoor phone booth. It wasn't an ideal location, but it was at least warm. I still couldn't fall asleep—I was too worried that someone would come and kick me out. I just sat there for hours, waiting—exhausted and lonely—for dawn to come. It was probably one of the longest and darkest nights of my life.

The next morning, I waited until breakfast time—due more to the cold than other factors. The pass was tough, but I knew I had to push through. I rode through until 2am; that's when I found the culvert pipes. With another brief rest, I hit the road, but the winds were once again not in my favor, nearly knocking me over several times. That's when I had to dig deep and find my faith.

God had done so much through the trip. I had left 140 days prior with $300 to my name and riding the wrong bicycle. I never ran out of money to the point of being in want. I had a new bike. I met new friends. I had seen the worst of humanity and I had flown miles above it all. I had more divine encounters daily over the course of 6100 miles than I had ever experienced before. I had prayed—and been prayed for—more than I ever had been before. And I learned more than anything, the less I worry, the more God shows up. I had realized it wasn't my bike—or even my trip—that God had been blessing. It was my faith and me seeing His glory that brought the blessing. God has his own plan and answered my prayers accordingly.

I don't know why that night in the pipes was so difficult. I'm sure a lot of it was exhaustion on every level: mental, physical, emotional, and spiritual. Everyone goes through difficult times. The situation reminded me of Psalm 23, "Even though I walk through the darkest valley, I will fear no evil, for you are with me; your rod and your staff, they comfort me." God had not brought me this far to leave me in these pipes. I had a destination and I had to get there. I couldn't turn around and go home. I couldn't call anyone to pick me up. I had to go forward.

My strength renewed and my purpose set in front of me, I called a Warm Showers stop just before the ferry to San Francisco. After being turned down so many times, it was nice to have Ed tell me I was welcome to stay with him. He also told me he had a couple other bicyclists staying with him. I took a shot and asked if it was Jesse and Royal. It was! I felt like God was actually testing me a little with this last day. I was getting a little crazy, but afterwards I had felt much better.

With the mental challenge behind me, the plan was to keep going to the end. There was a sense of irony to the whole rush. I was pushing to try to get to San Francisco, but I didn't really have a place to stay there. Regardless, it was only 50 miles—which was usually a cake walk. It quickly became the most challenging experience of the trip ... and thus probably the most challenging experience of my life.

This leg of the trip should have been a four hour ride, which meant I should have been eating lunch at a café in the City by the Bay. Instead, I was continuing to fight headwinds and hills. In fact, nine hours into the ride—twice what I had expected—I still had another 15 miles to go just to get to the ferry. After that, there was another hour's ride to San Francisco. The 30-40 mile an hour headwinds continued buffeting my spirit as well as my body. I'll admit the devil was bringing me down pretty hard. And I was at fault for letting him. It was just so insanely difficult, plus I had been pushing myself so hard the last few nights. I was already worn out. I stopped again and again, wanting to quit riding. At times the headwinds blew so strongly I couldn't ride. It was the closest I came to quitting the entire trip. I'd like to say something divine and amazing dropped out of the sky and pulled me through. I'd love to tell about the trucker with angel's wings that pulled over and towed me to the end. But in the end, I had to dig into my gut and find the strength to push through.

And then it hit me again—the verse that had carried me through so much of my trip: "I can do all this through [Christ] who gives me strength" (Php 4:13 NIV).

I'm glad I pushed through. I finally arrived at Ed's place to take advantage of the hospitality. Jesse and Royal showed up a little later. After we all cleaned up, Ed and his wife Dianne brought us pizza and made a warm apple pie. We woke up the next morning, enjoyed breakfast together, and then headed towards San Francisco.

It seemed so surreal—I only had five miles left to ride. After all the difficult days, it felt amazing. I hardly could get up to speed before we reached the ferry. I paid my fare, parked my bike, and let the boat carry me into the harbor. As I stood on the deck, looking around at the iconic Golden Gate Bridge over the bay, I was in complete awe.

Mike is ready to board the ferry that will take him to San Francisco

I couldn't believe I had actually made it: 6114 miles. I had started in Ohio, rode to Connecticut, down to Florida and west to California. I had lived the most incredible adventure.

Above: There's no mistaking the fog-obscured iconic Golden Gate

Below: Jesse, Royal, & Mike before their celebratory plunge

I wasn't done yet.

The adventure continued with Jesse's friend who bought us all lunch. Afterwards, we took our bikes down Lombard Street, enjoying the tight curves and steady downhill grade. Lombard Street was one of those sights that everyone associates with San Francisco and here I was snaking down it on my new bike. I was elated!

I also was a little nervous. I had $3.75 and no place to stay. I had contacted Warm Showers hosts but no one had returned my call. With nowhere else to turn, I thought I could just head to the park. I knew a lot of homeless people slept there, and—while I certainly wasn't homeless on a long-term basis, for all intents and purposes right now ... I was.

I still don't know why I don't just give all my worries to God. He always provides. Who was I to complain? God hadn't let me down ever—and certainly not since May 8th, when I started this trip. This would be no different.

After our ride, I called some people back home and asked them to pray for me. God, working on His schedule, answered those prayers in a big way. While we talked at dinner, Royal asked me if I wanted to go with him to Oregon to visit his sister. The best part was that he was not going on a bike; he was renting a van. We rode a train to the car rental and Royal bought me dinner.

The Journey Home

Above: Mike, Royal,
and their bikes enjoy
the speed, efficiency,
and comfort of a
train

Left: Cooking dinner
at Royal's family's
house

God blessed me with $50 from a friend back home, so I tried to repay Royal. He wouldn't let me. He called me a "brother in Christ" and he was glad to be able to help. His sister Jen cooked an amazing dinner.

The blessings kept coming while I was there. Friends back in Ohio actually bought my plane ticket as a surprise to my parents. I arrived at the airport at 10pm, though my flight didn't leave until 7am. The girl at the counter was nice enough to show me the best place in the airport to sleep. I didn't mind having to crash on the floor ... I knew tomorrow I would be back home in my room.

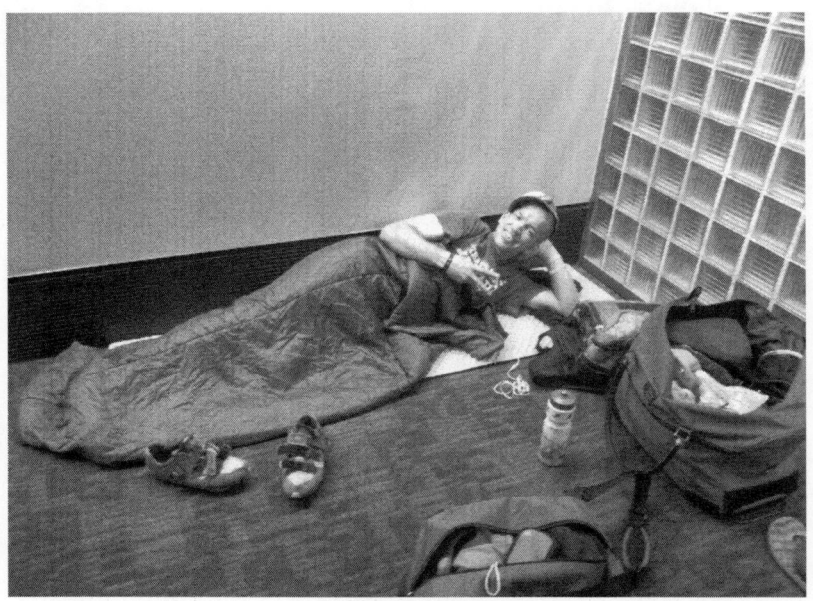

Mike's last night away from home, spent in the San Francisco airport

And so, with a combination of joy and sadness, it took me only a handful of hours to fly high above the country I had traversed. I didn't know what waited for me when I returned. Some things would be welcome and familiar: my home, my friends, and my family. Other things that were familiar would need to be changed. I thought about my work van, full of tools for my work in the labor industry. I wasn't sure I was ready to get back to that. It was a good industry and I could be helpful there. But I also felt God had something more for me. Like my trip, my job was a step to something I had never considered before. I had a brief thought: I might try to sell my tools. I realized that sometimes as human beings we need to be forced to do things. Left to our own, we embrace the *Rutyna Zabicia* and miss out on so much. My trip was a great example of this. I relied on God from start to finish because that was my only option. He always came through. So, if I sold my tools and totally started over, it would force me to get into a new line of work. That thought made me nervous, but I knew if I put my trust in God, He would never let me down. The one thing I was sure of, was that I couldn't have any doubts— either in myself or in the Lord.

With a sigh, I looked out the window of the jet. I knew that miles and miles below me were all the people I had met and the sights I had seen. And all around me was the God who carried me through it all: 300 dollars, a bike, 6114 miles, and 141 days.

Praise God.

23: AFTERWORD

Phil and Lila Baker, still unsure of how Mike was going to get home, were supposed to go out to dinner with their friends Roy and Melinda. The evening started out as predicted. Roy and Melinda picked up their friends. As Phil and Lila climbed into the vehicle, they saw a man sitting in the back seat. He looked scruffy and weathered, but there was no mistaking their son. Tears welling up in their eyes, the Bakers were reunited with their son after over a third of the year.

Later, Tom - the Baker's third son - would make a call to the bike shop in Searcy, Arkansas to buy a bike. Unlike the one Mike bought there, this one was worn. It was breaking down. The paint was scuffed. The whole thing had been in the rain, mud, and other elements. The tires were all wrong. In fact the whole bike had seen better days.

Mike's bikes - left: the one he started with; right: his new one

But it was Mike's bike—a testimony to the challenges he had overcome and the blessings God had provided. Mike certainly had some great stories to his trip. But put together, it was one great story about how everything worked out.

The story reinforced the Baker's faith in God. "There's generous people out there," Phil said, "but to come up at the exact moment Mike needs help? That's a miracle."

In fact, two things needed to happen. God was the orchestrator of the trip. He had to put Mike in the right places at the right time. But people, and their free will, still had the ability to choose to help or to pass by. In most cases those people had no idea who or what they were helping. "The people who helped Mike out," Phil said, "They probably didn't realize that by helping Mikey out—they were reaching hundreds and maybe thousands of people. You never know what's going to happen. And you shouldn't. You shouldn't do it to glorify yourself—do it to help other people."

Still, Phil thought more people needed to hear Mike's story.

There's one more "chance occurrence" that I need to add to this story, but I'm going to add it as myself and not as Michael. My name is Matthew Morgan and it's been my privilege to work with Mike on this book.

At the time we met one another, I was working at Gahanna Christian Academy in central Ohio as a high school Bible teacher. As my degree is in theology and pastoral ministries, I have sat through thousands of sermons in my lifetime. And when Michael came to our school to speak in our chapel service, I expected more of the same "3-point and a poem" sermons I'd heard. Michael, God bless him, was not among the most highly polished speakers I had heard. But he impressed me to the core of my being. He was genuine and real, and he held the attention of almost 200 middle school and high school students—not a small feat, since they are in chapel every week listening to different speakers. Anyway, Michael shared his heart and his stories, just as he had done through his bicycle trip. The students enjoyed his message and continued talking about him when they went to class.

Later that day, my principal, Chris Joseph, knocked at

my door and interrupted my class ... something I don't take kindly to (mostly due to my ADHD tendencies and trying to regain lost trains of thought). I knew if he was interrupting though, it must be important. I stepped into the hallway and he re-introduced me to Mike, explained a little of why he had taken me out of class, then went into my room to sit with my students while Mike and I talked. It turned out he and Chris had been talking most of the morning. Michael mentioned he had wanted to write a book about his trip. He had even started it, but he just wasn't sure where to go with it. And it just "happened" (as much as so many other things just "happened" on this trip), that Chris had a teacher on his staff who was also a writer ... me! At the time, I had just published my first novel ShadowLight and was in the middle of writing the sequel. Michael and I exchanged information and I told him I'd contact him over the summer, once I had finished the first draft of the sequel.

I finished that novel, and put it away to rest ... where it still sits to this day. Once I started this project, I didn't want to stop. We met—enjoying Chipotle together of course—and he handed me his journals and other information about the trip. I will admit I felt a strong sense of awe holding these two books. They went immediately into plastic bags and I was always careful as I read them. These had a lot of miles on them. For the entire summer, I poured over his journals, taking notes on everything—including transcribing many passages word-for-word. He gave me his YouTube channel information and I watched every single video he had uploaded, taking notes on each one ... and copying down many of his spoken thoughts verbatim as well. I wanted my words to be his, which in turn would come from God.

By the time I finished, I had felt like I had been with Mike for the entire trip. The truth is I know I would never be able to make a trip like Mike's—partly due to some physical limitations, and partly due to the simple fact that it wasn't my call. I could, however, live vicariously through him and his trip and let my faith grow as a result. And so my journey began there, following Mike after the fact and still being as blessed as he was through it.

The more I have thought about it though, I have taken a journey. Mike took it on a bike; I'm taking it through a book. Like Mike, I had to sacrifice some comforts. While I love my job, most people will agree that Christian school teachers do not join the profession for the money. I had been doing some writing on the side to bring in some income. However, I did not have enough time to do the side work and Mike's book. As summer began, I had to make a conscious decision whether to put Mike's book on the front burner or keep working the odd jobs to pay the bills. With the conviction that so many needed to hear this story—not just to hear about Mike, but also to come to a basic understanding of who God is, I let the side jobs lapse.

At first things were fine, but my wife, who has been unemployed since January 2011, had her unemployment checks end. She had been staying home with our then-six-month old son, which had been a blessing in itself, but it did not help the income issue. We seemed to constantly be losing money and having to tighten our belts. However God has always provided for us.

To my surprise (and yes, it shouldn't surprise me) God has taken care of all our needs. As money started to run tight and we weren't sure where our mortgage payment was going to come from, an old friend gave me $800 saying that God had told her to give me that money, making sure I knew that it wasn't from her. Other miracles from nowhere happened. At one point, my wife had a temporary job for a week, but we couldn't afford the gas to fill up the car. The Sunday before she started work (on Monday), someone at our church anonymously gave us $200 to Meijer—which just happens to have a gas station. We were able to fill up the car and afford groceries that week. We had only submitted a prayer request to the pastoral staff asking for prayer for our finances and God blessed us amazingly. He has even provided a good friend who has kept me well stocked on Starbucks to keep the concentration flowing. It was so amazing to see the blessings that Mike experienced flowing in my own life.

One of the things I appreciated most about Mike is his genuineness—he is who he appears to be. I could have easily doubled the size of this book if I had included every "praise God" he wrote or said during the trip. He had one of the most positive outlooks I have ever seen and kept it even in the most serious of circumstances. One of the best examples I saw of this was the video he recorded just after his accident in which he slipped, cut himself, and broke his new bike. The video opened with Michael laughing and smiling–not angry, not hurt, and not upset. It seemed to be ingrained in him—and that has caused me to try to seek to develop the same attitude in my own life.

I'm so grateful to Mike for allowing me to journey with him and for being so open to the tedium of the writing process. He has an amazing story and it is my privilege to be part of telling it.

Phil Baker, Sr. really said it best. "There's so much love that God has—we as Christians just need to share it. Go out and share the love. Be the Good Samaritan."

He's right. You'll never know how many people will be telling your story later. And we all have a story to tell.

~Matthew

INDEX OF WEB SITES:[1]

Achilles International - *www.achillesinternational.org*

The Adventure Cycling Association (ACA) -
http://www.adventurecycling.org

Coppola Photography - *www.coppolaphotography.com*

Food for the Hungry - *http://www.fh.org*

Give A Bike - *www.giveabike.com*

Matthew E. Morgan - *www.matthewEmorgan.com*

Michael T. Baker - *www.bikeforchrist.com*

Spot Satellite Messenger - *www.findmespot.com*

Warm Showers - *www.warmshowers.org*

World Bicycle Relief - *www.worldbicyclerelief.org*

---

[1] Note: No promotional consideration was given or intended for these sites

ABOUT THE AUTHOR

Michael T. Baker has owned his own remodeling/handyman business since 2008. After his trip across America on a bicycle, he returned to his business and has been extremely busy, blessed with more work than he could fathom.

In addition to his boom in employment, Michael also started a serious relationship after he returned. One year after their first date, Michael proposed to Sarah ... and she accepted.

Michael says that he and his wife could not be happier. Together they are planning to live out their lives serving God in whatever way possible.

Photo Courtesy of Brad Petersen

ABOUT THE CO-AUTHOR

Matthew E. Morgan studied theology, earning his BA in Biblical Studies from Trinity Bible College in Ellendale, ND. He has worked as a youth pastor, teacher, "technology guy," and an unfortunately-short stint as a stand-up comedian, while pursuing his Master of Arts in Professional Counseling from Liberty University in Lynchburg, VA.

Matthew has published one other full-length novel— ShadowLight, a young (and young at heart) adult speculative fiction novel. He has had numerous short stories and articles published as well.

His favorite accomplishment, however, is coming home every day to his faithful wife, Martha and his beautiful son, Michael—who is still just young enough to be called beautiful.

11104480R00173

Made in the USA
San Bernardino, CA
07 May 2014